PHILOSOPHY

Thinking about Meaning

JOHN WILSON

*Director of the Farmington Trust
Research Unit, Oxford*

HEINEMANN EDUCATIONAL BOOKS
LONDON

Heinemann Educational Books Ltd
LONDON EDINBURGH MELBOURNE AUCKLAND TORONTO
SINGAPORE HONG KONG KUALA LUMPUR
IBADAN NAIROBI JOHANNESBURG
LUSAKA NEW DELHI

012 5092

170285

ISBN 0 435 46180 X ✔

87582

Key Book
Ref
100
WIL

Published in Great Britain by
Heinemann Educational Books Ltd
48 Charles Street, London W1X 8AH
Printed Offset Litho and bound by
Cox & Wyman Ltd, London, Fakenham and Reading

CONCEPT BOOKS

General Editor: Alan Harris

CONCEPT BOOKS · 1

PHILOSOPHY—*Thinking about Meaning*

Contents

Preface

THIS book is an introduction to a particular kind of thinking. Various high-sounding, abstract, academic and more or less mysterious names have been given to it: 'semantics', 'conceptual analysis', 'linguistic philosophy', and so on. It is in fact an introduction to *philosophical* thinking, in that sense of 'philosophical' which has been current in universities over the last thirty or forty years. The words 'philosophy' and 'philosophical' are apt to put people off, because they are supposed to stand for something very 'abstract' and difficult, which could only be done by advanced students of high intelligence. This may have been true of old-style philosophy, but it has not been true since about 1930.

The kind of philosophical thinking now current does not involve the student in a profound study of Plato, Descartes, and Kant; nor in the complexities of formal logic; nor yet in those complex metaphysical problems often put under such headings as 'the meaning of life', 'ultimate reality', and so forth. It is very different from all of these. Essentially it is informal, and a matter of learning to talk and think in a certain way. Anybody can do it; there is little if any correlation between students of high 'academic standards' (as we too often misguidedly say) and students who can do it well.

It is a great pity that the general public – and this may well include many teachers – are not clear about what sort of thing this kind of thinking is, or what 'philosophy' really means. This is largely the fault of professional philosophers, who have not been very good at making it plain. The second part of the Introduction to this book will, I hope (together with the chapters which follow), give you some idea of what we shall be trying to do, if you are not already certain. All I want to do here is to combat a number of common prejudices – that all 'philosophy' is very difficult, that it can't be taught to young people, or that it is all too 'abstract' to be of much use anyway. Nobody who has done any proper philosophy should share these prejudices, and one purpose in writing the book is to try to remove them.

Although this book was written primarily for the benefit of students at school, it would be a mistake to think that the needs of this particular class of students are substantially different from the needs of any other beginners in philosophy. If the book has any merit, it ought to be helpful not just for students and teen-agers, but for anybody who has yet to take the first steps in this kind of thinking. Adults who want to develop this skill will find that they may learn less from 'grown-up' books on philosophy than they suppose. It is fatally easy to turn the pages of some advanced work on the subject, and imagine that one has learnt something.

Very often adults who claim to have done some philosophy ask me the question, 'What is *your* philosophy, Mr Wilson?', a ques-tion which shows only too plainly that they haven't even taken the first step of grasping what sort of activity philosophy is. They still think in terms of *a* philosophy : some way of life, creed, or view of reality which philosophers try to sell, rather than in terms of a special kind of thinking. To ask, 'What is your philosophy?' is as silly as to ask 'What is your history?' or 'What is your science?'

I should be sorry if this kind of thinking were learnt or taught simply because the word 'philosophy' has cultural overtones, or because teachers thought that their pupils should be 'cultured'. Philosophy is far more important than that. It is an essential tool for dealing with practical problems, for nearly all important practical problems – in morality, religion, politics, personal rela-tionships and many other areas – depend on clarity in this kind of thinking: that is, on *conceptual* clarity. Just as all pupils need to be taught to think in a manner appropriate to science, in another manner appropriate to morality and personal relationships, in another appropriate to history, and so forth, so they all need to be taught about *meaning* – about the words and concepts we use. This skill is essential to them as human beings, and is worth infinitely more than a superficial knowledge of Plato or Bertrand Russell.

I should also be sorry if any teacher felt incapable of teaching philosophy just because he was not expert in it. Philosophy is not that kind of subject; indeed, it is not a subject in the usual sense at all. It is rather a certain kind of communication, in which both teacher and taught share in a dialogue. In an important sense, we are all students or learners in philosophy : some people are better at it than others, but there are no experts, in the way that there are experts in science or history or mathematics. It is not a matter of taking notes or memorizing facts, but a matter of learning to talk and think in a particular kind of way : to talk and think about *meaning*.

I think it will be found that this skill fits in very well with a large number of educational objectives : not only, for instance, with the whole concept of 'straight thinking', 'oral expression' or 'the use of English', but with the general moral education of the pupil, and his ability in personal relationships. It may naturally be supplemented by other kinds of thinking of a more factual nature, such as those kinds of thinking which come under such (perhaps equally 'academic') titles as 'psychology' or 'sociology'. If it is to be fruitful, philosophy has to be understood in its own right for what it is. But I hope very much that teachers will not be hesitant or uncertain about putting other such subjects in general on the educational map. For they are *not* merely academic play-things, suitable only for the minds of university dons or winners of open scholarships; they are basic human skills, which will only improve our society and the individuals in it if teachers succeed in imparting them to the rising generation.

J. B. W.
Farmington Trust Research Unit
Oxford
1967

Introduction

Why Bother to Think?

THIS book is supposed to help people to think in certain ways, but I do not believe it will be of much use unless I start by making it plain why thinking is important and why it is difficult. By 'thinking' I don't mean just day-dreaming, or remembering, or wanting, or fearing, or having a feeling about something. I mean something more like using your brain, using words or other symbols to find an answer. Thinking is something which men do and most animals don't. Most animals do all sorts of complicated things, but what they do is dictated to them by their instincts. They can't *think about* what they're doing, or make plans, or change their behaviour, or ask and answer questions. They just carry on doing whatever they do. But human beings have the power to forget what they're doing for the minute; they can take a mental step backwards, as it were, and consider whether what they're doing is right or wrong, sensible or stupid.

Just as human beings can stop doing things and think about doing them, so too they can stop saying things and think about what they're saying. They can wonder whether what they're saying is true or false, likely or unlikely, reasonable or unreasonable. This is what happens in arguments. If I say 'The earth's flat' and you say 'No, it's round', and we both just go on saying this over and over again, we can't get an argument started. The argument can only start when one of us stops saying 'It's flat' or 'It's round', and begins to give *reasons* or offer *evidence*. Very young children who just say to each other 'It is', 'It isn't', 'It is', 'It isn't', and go on saying so, aren't arguing and aren't thinking. It's only when they say things like 'I think it is, *because* . . .' that they start thinking. But to say such things means putting their own views on one side for the time being, and very young children find this difficult.

As a matter of fact all human beings find this difficult, not only children. Men have always disliked thinking, because it's hard work, and it's much easier not to bother. For many thousands of years men progressed at a snail's pace, doing exactly what their fathers had done, using primitive flint tools, living off what they could find in the way of roots and berries and the animals they could catch. Only very late in human history did they discover or invent things like the use of metals, agriculture, or reading and writing. Although these things are obviously useful, and don't really demand all that much intelligence to invent, they found it easier to go on doing what they had always done.

This is still true today. Although there are all sorts of highly developed arts and sciences, people still think only when they have to. And people seem capable of putting up with an awful lot of difficulties before they feel that they must really start thinking about them and solving the necessary problems. We have very serious problems about war, and disease, and starvation, and insanity, and unhappiness, but we still don't spend much time thinking about them. We're prepared to complain about them, or to say how shocking they are, or we may even be willing to rush in and do something about them. But what we do may be mistaken, and we can't tell whether it is unless we think first.

The point of thinking, then, is simply that thinking is useful. It gets us what we want. It isn't just something which you are supposed to do at school because the teacher expects it, or because you have to pass exams, or because thinking is an 'educated' or 'cultural' or 'scholarly' thing to do. Quite a lot of people believe that they somehow ought to be 'intellectual' or 'cultural' – that it's more respectable or more upper-class if they pretend to enjoy reading books about history or philosophy. In the same way lots of people believe they ought to like classical music rather than pop music, because it makes them feel more cultured. But in fact if philosophy and other subjects which make you think are any good at all, they must have some point, or purpose, or use; just as, if classical music is more worth listening to than pop music, it must be because it has more to offer and gives more pleasure.

The difficulty with thinking (and perhaps with classical music too, by the way) is that it doesn't pay immediate dividends. You start by having a problem, and you have to resist the temptation to try to solve it too quickly. In order to solve it, you may need all sort of techniques and ideas which don't, at first sight, seem to be connected with the problem in any obvious way. For instance, there are still some primitive peoples who build their bridges with immense labour out of plaited reeds and creepers. In order to teach them how to build proper bridges, which will bear a person's weight without collapsing, you have to teach them a bit of elementary mathematics. But this is very difficult : not because the mathematics itself is particularly hard, but because the primi-tive people don't see the point of it. They have to stop building their bridges the old way, and start learning things like the multi-plication tables, which seem to them completely pointless and nothing to do with bridges at all.

Now of course this seems silly to us : but only because we know how mathematics is connected with bridge-building. There are plenty of techniques and ways of thinking which we often take to be pointless or silly, or a waste of time, or 'academic', or 'too abstract', but which are in fact essential for solving the problems we have. These are just the things that the primitive peoples say about mathematics; and indeed mathematics is, in a sense, an 'abstract' or 'academic' subject – only we couldn't get very far without it. Mathematics isn't as immediately exciting as flying aeroplanes, but without mathematics there wouldn't be any aero-planes to fly.

Because thinking is hard work, we put up all sorts of resistances and defences against having to do it. Saying that it's 'too abstract' or 'academic' is only one of them. Another very common one is to say something like 'Oh, well, it's all a matter of taste anyway'. This is frequently said when the subject under discussion is something like morals or religion. We sometimes believe it's just a matter of individual choice whether to have a religion or none at all, or to have this or that moral code. But is it? Religious believers don't think it is, and nearly all of us think that some ways of behaving (like murder, for instance) really are wrong. In any case, we should have to think quite hard to settle the question of whether these things are matters of taste or not. What's really in our minds when we say this sort of thing is: 'The whole thing is so difficult, I just can't face finding out what's true or false, and right or wrong, so let's drop the subject'.

Another reaction – another way of defending ourselves against thinking – is to say things like 'Reason can only get you so far; after that you have to make a leap of faith', or 'You have to rely on intuition.' This is really only a rather stronger version of the last defence we looked at. It says, in effect, that just because you believe something, that by itself makes what you believe right or true. A lot of words, like 'faith', or 'revelation', or 'intuition', are used to cover up this idea, which in its naked form is obviously silly, and there are a great many occasions on which people say things like, 'Well, you may argue as much as you like, but I just *know* that . . .', or 'I just *feel* that . . .'. What is missing here is the notion of *giving reasons* for beliefs. If we abandon this notion, there is really nothing to distinguish sane human beings from lunatics. What makes a lunatic is that he believes something but has no good reason for believing it. To be willing to give reasons, to have your beliefs out in public, to allow them to be inspected and challenged, is essential for all kinds of thinking.

Yet another defence is to say something like 'Well, it all depends what you've been brought up to believe, doesn't it?', the idea being that if, for instance, you've been brought up to believe that there is a God, or that sleeping with people before you're married is wrong, that settles it; there isn't any need to think about it. But of course, although obviously how you've been brought up does in fact make a great difference to what you believe, it doesn't give you good *reasons* for believing it. If some Nazi who'd been brought up to kill Jews said, 'Oh, well, I was brought up that way, there's no point our arguing about it', we shouldn't accept this as a defence. Indeed, we should think that he was doubly wrong : first, he was wrong about how to treat Jews, and second – which is really far worse, when you come to think about it – he isn't open to argument. He's resigned from being a reasonable human being; he's no longer open to criticism, or able to change his mind. He is not very far from being mad.

It should already be plain that the business of thinking is best done *in public*, that's to say, in the process of discussion, cross-questioning, arguing, giving reasons, and so forth. This is because being reasonable, or thinking correctly, is a public matter and not a private one : it must stand up to public inspection. It's no good saying 'Well, I have my own ideas on this, and my own feelings, and that's good enough for me.' If it's really good for you, then it must be capable of being shown to other people. It's true that some ways of life or some beliefs may suit certain people, and not suit others, just as some drugs may benefit some men and harm others. But it's also true that you can be right or wrong about what beliefs suit your particular temperament, just as you can be right or wrong about what drugs suit your body, and this makes it a public matter, not just a matter of taste.

Even when you think on your own, or when you're reading a book (like this one), you're really conducting a sort of cross-talk with yourself or with the author of the book. If you have any kind of problem which you're trying to solve, you say to yourself something like, 'Well, there's this point, but then again, what about that one? Now supposing this were true, what difference would it make? But is there any evidence that it is true? Let's look at it from another angle : suppose . . .' and so on. This is like what goes on when a group of people discuss something, and it goes on in your own head when you're thinking by yourself. Thinking and talking, or expressing yourself, are very closely connected; indeed they're almost the same.

It isn't surprising, then, that most of our weaknesses in thinking come out most obviously when we're discussing with other people. Some people are so nervous or frightened of making fools of themselves that they stay silent, and don't dare to express themselves. Other people are so keen on their own views that they keep repeating them over and over again, without listening to the views of other people. Some people interrupt when others are talking; other people get angry if their opinions are challenged, and turn the discussion into a row. Some people are over-cautious, and try to be absolutely sure that they're right before they say anything; other people are rash, and just charge ahead with their ideas before they've got them properly sorted out. And all of us, above all, need a great deal of practice. It takes young children quite a few years to learn to talk at all, and when we are older, not many of us get to the stage where we can talk properly – where we can conduct a rational conversation, which is more than just gossip or a conventional chat and also which isn't a slanging match.

Teaching people to talk and think is one of the most important things that parents and schools ought to do, and I'm afraid that they don't always do it very well, so that people lack the necessary practice. Because people aren't used to it, they don't realize that it's one of the most exciting and interesting activities there are. They are not very good at thinking, and thinking is quite difficult anyway, so they more or less give up trying. They have a few rather sketchy views about life, or God, or politics, or morals, or marriage, which they've learnt either by taking them direct from their parents or by reacting violently against their parents; they've not had them submitted to any real questioning or criticism. As they get older, they get less and less inclined to think, and begin more and more to act and talk like robots or puppets, just going through the motions of life without really questioning and examining the world around them. Sometimes one feels that they might as well be dead, and this is rather frightening.

Thinking is not really an *intellectually* difficult thing to do. You don't require a very high I.Q., or need to know a vast number of facts. It's a skill, like learning to walk or to swim or to play a game. What you need is patience, and plenty of practice.

But it helps a great deal if you have the incentive, and in this book I've tried to pick those subjects which my readers may already regard as practical problems which require an answer. Strictly speaking, this shouldn't be necessary : remember the case of the primitive bridge-builders, where the apparently 'abstract' or 'academic' subject of mathematics in fact turned out to be absolutely vital to their own problems. But it is a help if we start with something which obviously needs a solution – something which it will be useful for us to get straight about. People have different interests and different worries, and some of the things I've chosen may still seem remote to some people, but I've done the best I can.

One last thing that I must emphasize. Books by themselves aren't much good. There's as much resistance to them – and for the same reasons – as there is to thinking. Somebody can read a book, and say, 'Well, that's quite interesting', and it may have had no effect on him whatsoever. This is because he hasn't had to do any work himself; he's read the words, but perhaps hasn't bothered to think about them – to criticize them, argue about them, and so on. If you don't do this, books are a bore, and this is probably why so few people read them. But a book can help as a starting-off point – so long as the author doesn't try to do your thinking *for* you, but simply tries to *make* you think. This isn't easy, and the author is often tempted to do too much : to give you too much of his views, and express himself at too great a length. So what I've done is to write comparatively little on each subject, and produce some questions to answer. After that – indeed, I hope, during it as well – you need to argue amongst yourselves and with other people. It helps to make yourself write things down, because by doing this you can gain a clear idea of what you really think, and then you can show it to somebody who will criticize it for you, and help you to get clearer. There is of course a great deal written about all these subjects, and at the end I've put a list of books which it would be useful to read. But there would be no point in doing this unless you've already acquired the habit of thinking and arguing. You've got to want to know before you have any chance of finding out. You've got to be able to tolerate doubt, and uncertainty, and not being sure whether you're right, and you've got to learn to take and give criticism in public.

Thinking About Meaning

If you want one word for what this book is about, the right word is philosophy'; but it is quite likely that you will have the wrong idea of what philosophy is (if indeed you have any idea at all). I don't want to spend much time explaining this, because the only way to learn is really to *do* some philosophy, which you will be doing in this book. But a few points may be useful.

First, 'philosophy' is just a name for a special kind of thinking, and after what we've said already we ought to have a fairly clear idea about what thinking is. By 'a special kind of thinking' I *don't* mean thinking about a special subject or topic. For example, we can study the history of the nineteenth century, or the twentieth century : these are different topics or subjects, but the same kind of thinking – historical thinking – is needed for both. I mean rather thinking in a special kind of *way*.

Different ways of thinking are required in order to answer different kinds of questions. A question like 'What happened to cause the Second World War?' demands historical thinking : we need to know the facts, to try and piece together what went on in the minds of people like Hitler and Churchill, and so forth. A question like, 'Why does the earth go round the sun?' demands scientific thinking : we have to do experiments, observe certain things carefully, and so on. Philosophical thinking is a special kind, just as these are, but it is very different in nature.

Philosophical thinking is thinking about *meaning*. The questions that call for it may be obviously about meaning, such as, 'What do we mean when we talk about "democracy", or "justice", or "a work of art"?' But often the questions are *disguised*. Someone might ask, 'What is truth?', or, 'Is there an absolute right or wrong?', or, 'Are all men really equal?' These *look* like questions of fact : 'What is truth?' may look like 'What is a zebra?', or 'What is the French for "horse"?' But really they are questions of meaning. We should have to find out how the words in the questions – 'truth', 'justice', 'right', 'wrong', 'equal', etc. – are actually used in our everyday speech.

You might think that we know this already, or that if we didn't we could just look them up in a dictionary. But this is at best only half-true. In a sense we know how to use the words; that is, we usually use them correctly when we talk. But *we don't know the rules which govern their use*. This is why it is so hard to give simple and correct definitions of them; for the rules, which we unconsciously follow when we talk, are often in fact very complicated and difficult to sketch. This is also why dictionaries are not much help: they can only give very short answers which don't really settle the matter.

Philosophical thinking is chiefly a matter of becoming clearer about the rules which govern the use of certain words and statements, that is, about meaning. This sounds simple, but it isn't. It needs an awful lot of hard work, patience, concentration, and sensitivity to the use of language. At the same time, it's often much more exciting and rewarding than other kinds of thinking – particularly the kinds where you have to learn lots of facts. There are no facts in philosophy, or, if there are, they are facts about the way words are used. And these facts one has to discover for oneself; they aren't the kind of facts you can write down in a textbook and memorize.

Part of the excitement in philosophy, in my opinion, is because most of the interesting questions in life are philosophical ones, or, at least, call for some philosophical thinking before we can start to answer them. Questions about religion, morals, art, politics, psychology, crime, sex, the family and many other important – and very practical – topics, nearly always have philosophical implications. For example, people have been arguing for thousands of years about whether there's a God and whether certain things are morally right and wrong. But they haven't got very far, because until recently they didn't use philosophical thinking; they didn't ask *what it meant to say* that there was a God or that something was morally right. These are words and phrases that people use every day, but without being clear about what they mean.

Only in the last thirty or forty years has it become generally agreed that philosophers ought to be concerned with meaning (and not, for instance, with laying down moral codes of their own, or trying to find out facts as if they were scientists). This doesn't at all mean that what philosophers in the past have written is boring or useless. Indeed, philosophy began with Socrates and Plato over two thousand years ago; it was when Socrates made the first all-important step of asking the ancient Athenians questions like, 'But what do you mean by "virtue"?' (or 'courage', or 'justice', or almost anything) that human beings first began to question, criticize, and think about meaning. The step consists essentially of *thinking about what you're saying*. A man starts doing philosophy when he stops just talking and thinks about what he means by his talk. Philosophy is talk about talk.

For this reason philosophy isn't something that can be split up into completely different topics, in the sort of way that we can split science up into chemistry, biology, physics, etc. It is a skill, a type of thinking, that we can apply to *any* situation where language is used. Of course, problems about meaning crop up more in some areas than in others; hence we can talk, if we like, about 'the philosophy of morals', or 'the philosophy of religion'. We wouldn't talk about 'the philosophy of fishmongering', because (as far as I know) no problems about the meaning of words crop up while selling fish.

For the same reason too, anyone can do philosophy, just as anyone can learn to swim or to ride a bicycle; some people may be naturally better than others at it, but it's mostly a question of how much practice you have, and how interested you are. You don't have to know anything to start with; this is partly an advantage, because you can start doing it straight away, though for some people it is worrying, because there aren't any facts to cling on to. It gets progressively easier as you go on, and it shouldn't take very long to get the hang or the 'feel' of this kind of thinking.

Once you've got it, a whole new country opens before you. But rather than go on trying to explain what philosophy* is, it will be better to do some.

---

* Of course the word 'philosophy' isn't *only* used to describe the kind of skills and the kind of thinking that we've been talking about here. It's also used – particulary in European countries – to describe quite different kinds of skills and thinking. We shan't be concerned with these different kinds in this book, so there's no need for me to explain them at this point, but the reader can learn a bit more about this topic at the end of the book (pp. 107–10).

I
CONCEPTS IN
RELIGION, MORALITY
AND ART

one

Religion

RELIGION IS quite a good subject to start with, because it's something that everybody knows something about and is familiar with, and yet something which hardly anybody ever *thinks* about. What happens, in most parts of the world, is that some people take sides – either you are a firmly-believing Christian or else you feel strongly that Christianity is a lot of nonsense that ought to be stopped – and other people are so bored with the whole thing that they've stopped asking whether it's true a long time ago. All these reactions are understandable, but they aren't reasonable. It's no good pretending to be sure that religion is right or that it's wrong, since there are obviously lots of intelligent people on both sides, and it can't be as easy to settle as all that; and it's no good just thinking that it's a matter of taste, since for all we know it might be both true and important, as some religious people say it is. So we have to think.

The first thing to think about is what religion is supposed to *be*, and the best question to ask is, 'When Christians (or other religious believers) say that there's a God, or that God answers prayer, or that we ought to do what Christ tells us, what *sort* of thing are they saying?' The point of the question is this: when somebody tells us that there are men on Mars or that water changes to ice, we know more or less what he means – we may or may not agree, but at least we understand him. But when somebody tells us that there's a God, or a life after death, or that the bread and wine in the communion service change into the body and blood of Christ, I think our first reaction ought to be, 'What do you mean?'

This is an important point, not only for this subject but for many others. People say lots of things which we don't really understand (although we often think we do, because what they say sounds like a sensible English sentence), and which perhaps the people who say them don't really understand either. When someone says 'There's a God', we find it natural to reply by saying either 'I agree' or 'I don't agree', or perhaps 'Well, you can think that if you like, I don't care.' But all these replies are wrong, because *it's not clear what he means*. We don't really know that he means *anything* – it's quite possible for people to put words together in an English sentence without their really meaning anything at all, and it's very common for them to think that they mean one sort of thing, and really mean another.

Let me try to make this clear by an example. If I said 'Smith always answers when you speak to him', or 'Mother always gives you something to eat when you ask for it', you know what I mean because you know what counts as 'answering' or 'giving'. You can check up on what I say by listening to what happens when you speak to Smith, or seeing what happens if you ask mother for some food. You'd know how to test the truth of what I said – even if you couldn't test it immediately (perhaps because Smith was a difficult person to get hold of, or mother was busy). But now suppose I say 'God answers prayer'. You go away and pray, and say 'O God, answer me this question, or give me that thing', and nothing happens. You don't hear a voice, or get the thing, or if you do get the thing, you see no reason to believe that it was God – you might have got it by luck, or by hard work, or from a friend. Then – and this is the point – if I keep on saying 'Well, God *does* answer prayer', and you keep on trying and nothing happens, you ought to begin to wonder what I mean by 'answer'. 'Answer' in English usually means speaking or communicating in some way that you could test or check up on, by listening to a voice or receiving a parcel or something. But even though there are no voices and no parcels, I still go on saying 'God answers prayer'. And now it's not clear that I really mean *anything* by the word 'answer'.

Take another example : 'Water changes to ice' is comprehensible because we have some experience which we can use to test the truth of the remark. We see some sloshy wet stuff, which is what 'water' means, and then we see the same stuff become hard and very cold, which is what 'ice' means, and because we've seen the same stuff become different in certain respects we can say, in English, that it's 'changed'. That's what 'changed' means. But now if I say 'The bread and wine change into the body and blood of Christ', what can I mean? If you test the bread and wine before and after the communion service, it appears to be exactly the same; there isn't any test which would show any change in it at all. So now, what you ought to say is something like, 'Look, the word "change" in English is only comprehensible if there's some observable difference in things before and after; so when you say that the bread and wine "changes", and then say that there's no detectable difference in it, you seem to be contradicting yourself – you don't seem to mean *anything* by the word "change" '.

You should now be able to see the real difficulty with religious talk. The real difficulty isn't to know whether it's true or false, but what it can possibly *mean*. You can ask religious people what they mean, but I personally don't think that they have given any clear reply on this point. This may show that they don't mean anything – that they're just stringing words together for their own amusement – or it might show that they mean something different from what they appear to mean. This is the problem.

Go back to our original question, 'When people say there's a God, what *sort* of thing are they saying?' What we have just done, in a rather slapdash way, is this : we have investigated one possibility, the possibility that, in saying 'There's a God' and other such things, they intend to *give information* or *state facts*. Certainly this looked like a reasonable interpretation, because 'There's a God', looks like 'There are men on Mars', or 'There's a planet called Jupiter', and both of these statements give information. But now we are beginning to doubt whether this is the right interpretation after all, because as soon as you start asking for evidence for there being a God, or God answering prayer, the religious person says in effect that there isn't any. There don't seem to be any tests by which you could prove such statements true or false. So perhaps the statements don't really give any information at all – perhaps they do some other job, such as expressing the feelings of the people who make the statements. This would make them more like pieces of poetry, which aren't intended to state facts but to express and arouse feelings.

A lot of believers would object to this, and since it's a crucial point we must try to state it a bit more clearly. What's really wrong with these statements, if we take them to be giving information, is that *there's no way they could be proved wrong*. To use a technical term, they're not *falsifiable*. And this shows that the words in the statement don't really have the meaning they look as if they had. To take another example: if I said 'There's a little man flying round the room' and then added, 'but you can't see him or hear him or touch him, and indeed there's absolutely no way in which you could prove that he was there or that he wasn't there', you should reply 'Well, then, in that case I can't see what you could possibly *mean* by "little man" and "flying around", because these phrases are only comprehensible by reference to some sort of experience which would test the truth of what you said; if you allow *nothing*, no observation of any kind, to disprove your statement, then you can't be stating facts. Perhaps what you want to say is that it feels to you as if there's a little man, or you feel impelled to believe that there is, or that you're suffering from some sort of hallucination, or something of that kind.'

But now, if religion isn't intended to give us information or state facts, what is it? Well, perhaps it's just a rather special way of advocating and following a moral code or a way of life. Perhaps when religious people say 'God is our father; so we ought to love each other as brothers', what they really mean is 'We ought to love each other as brothers : so it's helpful to pretend (so to speak) that there's a loving father who has created us all.' On this view the statements of religion that seem to state facts would really be giving a kind of myth, or story, or imaginative picture which is a useful backing to a certain way of life. It might well be convenient to *pretend* that there's a God of a certain kind, if you think that a certain way of life is good.

There are plenty of examples of this kind of thing. Thus, when people say 'All men are equal', or 'All men are born free', it looks as if they were stating facts. But if you come to think of it, what facts can they possibly state? All men plainly aren't equal in any respect; they have different shapes and sizes, different degrees of intelligence, different abilities, and so forth. What these people really want to say is something like 'We ought to treat people equally or fairly', or 'People should be left as free as possible'. These are very reasonable moral views, but they aren't facts; they don't give any information about what is the case, they just say what ought to be. But it sounds more impressive if you pretend that there's some sort of supernatural or marvellous truth which backs your moral code, and so there's a temptation to say, 'All men are equal' as if you were stating a fact.

To have myths or stories of this kind, which aren't strictly true, but which are convenient or useful for living in certain ways, isn't as bad as it may sound. It's something which we all do. If you're patriotic, you look on the Queen or the national flag as something special; the Queen is more than just an ordinary person, and the flag is more than just a piece of cloth with colours on. If you're in love, the person you're in love with is more than just another human begin; he (or she) is marvellous, attractive, almost super-human, and so on. Of course you know, if you like to put it that way, that he isn't really all that different from other people, but you find yourself talking and acting as if he was. And this may not be silly. It may be useful for getting something achieved, like perhaps marriage or bringing up a family.

So what religious people ought to say, perhaps, is not 'This is the undoubted, provable truth – that there's a loving God who made us, etc., etc.', but rather 'This is the way you ought to look at the world – *as if* it were the creation of a loving God, etc., etc.' What they are offering is not a set of facts, but (so to speak) a pair of spectacles through which you can look at the world, and they claim that this pair of spectacles brings better results. Perhaps it comforts people, or keeps them saner, or gives them fuller and richer lives, or makes them feel that life has some point and meaning.

But now, if we wonder whether to have a religion or not, or what religion to have, we shall look at the matter in a very different way. We shall look at the sort of results that different religions have. These results will not only be social – we shall not only ask questions like, 'Has the Church done more harm than good?' or 'Did the Roman Catholic Church hold up the progress of science in the Middle Ages?', but also questions like 'Does religion stop people from being over-anxious?' or 'Does being a Roman Catholic help to keep you sane?'

In general it is fairly obviously true that different psychological types of people tend to follow different religions. If you are the sort of person that needs to accept a fairly strict authority, you may well find the Roman Catholic Church suits you, for in that Church you are told to believe and do a greater number of things than in most other churches. If, on the other hand, you like to make up your own mind more often, but still like some kind of authority, then you might belong to some low-church sect. This applies to other outlooks and creeds which may not be really religions, but share a great many things in common with religion : Communism is an obvious example. People who follow the Party line in Communism clearly like being under authority, just as Roman Catholics do.

This still does not mean that it is a matter of taste what religion (if any) you have. You may instinctively feel that you like, or dislike, being under an authority, and you may feel pleased or angry or bored by certain religious rituals, like going to church, or confessing, or praying. But this doesn't prove that it actually *suits* you. It may be some weakness in you that makes you feel that way. Thus, whatever you feel about authority, it may be that the acceptance of some kind of authority is absolutely necessary to remain sane and not be anxious all the time; or alternatively it may be that the acceptance of authority cripples your mental

development and makes you more worried than you would otherwise be.

On this view of religion, then, the question must depend on the
facts about the mental make-up of human beings. Psychologists
are divided on this point. Some, like Freud, believe that the desire
for religion, for worship and belief in a God, is a mental weakness
which ought to be cured, and perhaps can be; others, like Jung,
believe that it is a mark of sanity, and an essential part of being
human. I don't think it can really be settled until we know a good
deal more about human psychology. But meanwhile we can say,
of course, that certain types of religions – and also some anti-
religious views – seem rather insane. Somebody who feels he has
to burn people at the stake for being irreligious cannot be really
happy in himself, and somebody who feels that he has to laugh at
parsons all the time can't be either.

It is a pity that religious people themselves have not really tried
to get clear about which sort of thing religion is – whether it's an
attempt to tell the truth, state facts or give information about some
'supernatural world' which really exists, or whether it's a kind of
way of looking at the world which is supposed to be psychologically beneficial. Most orthodox religion is really based on the
first interpretation, but recently people like the Bishop of
Woolwich seem to have taken the second view. In other words,
when religious people talk about God, we want to know
whether they're supposed to be talking about some person who
is really there, quite apart from human feelings and desires, or
whether they're talking in a special way *about* human feelings and
desires. 'God' could be the name of some super-being in heaven,
or just another word for 'love' or 'what you find deep in the human
heart'.

I think myself that religion, if it's to make sense at all, must be
one or the other of these two things. But we shouldn't be in too
much of a hurry to say this. Religion has often been used to give
answers to a number of questions which human beings have asked
for thousands of years, questions which don't really seem to fit
either interpretation : that is, they don't seem to be either

questions about facts, or questions about human feelings. Some of these questions are : 'Who made everything?', 'What is the meaning of life?', 'What are we all here for?', 'What is the reason for the existence of the universe?', 'Why is everything as it is?' God is often brought in as an answer to these questions – indeed some religions claim to prove that there is a God, because these questions (they think) must have an answer, and the only answer can be God.

Now there is something funny about all these questions, and they are a good example of a situation in which people think they are talking sense, when in fact they are either not talking sense at all, or talking a different kind of sense from what they think. Take a question like, 'What is the purpose of everything?' Now it's sense to ask what the purpose of a particular thing is, because we can answer it by reference to other things in the world. We can answer, 'What's the purpose of a hammer?' by talking about something outside the hammer, like nails and bits of wood, and we say, 'Its purpose is to knock nails into bits of wood.' And we can go on asking what the purpose of nails is – what nails are for – and give an answer referring to house-building or something like that. And we can go further and ask what houses are for, and say, 'So that men can have shelter.' And so on. But if we say, 'What's the purpose of everything?' or, 'What's it *all* for?' it isn't an intelligible question, because we've left ourselves nothing that we could use for an answer. 'Everything', or 'the universe', has nothing outside it which we could quote as a purpose.

'Who made everything?' is a silly question too. First, it contains some assumptions that may not be true : it assumes that some*body* rather than some*thing* made everything, and it also assumes that everything was made, and didn't just happen. But what makes it really silly is that if the word 'everything' really includes absolutely *everything*, then it can't possibly have an answer. You can say, 'God made everything', if by 'everything' you really mean 'everything but God', but then you can go on to ask, 'Who made God?' The objection to the question here is the same as the objection to questions like, 'What is the purpose of everything?', i.e. these questions aren't answerable because they leave no room for an answer.

This isn't to say that such questions are nonsensical. They may make some kind of sense, but not the same kind as ordinary sensible questions like, 'What's the purpose of a hammer?' or, 'Who made that hammer?' The answer may be that they aren't really *questions*, even though they have question-marks at the end. For instance, suppose it's Monday morning, and I have a bad head-ache and don't feel much like facing life, I might say, 'Oh, lord, what's it all for?' But I wouldn't really be expecting an answer; what I would be meaning is something like, 'Oh, lord, I don't really feel like doing anything much', or, 'Nothing seems very attractive today'. I'd be expressing my feelings, even though I used the form of a question.

Hence when people say things like, 'There's got to be a first cause for the universe', or, 'Somebody must have started the whole thing off', or, 'Life must have some purpose to it', we must be careful about words like 'got to be' and 'must'. There isn't any logical or rational necessity about it; indeed, as I've tried to show already, there wouldn't be any sense in saying that 'everything' had a cause or a purpose. 'Got to be' and 'must' surely represent a psychological feeling which some people have; they feel that it's somehow psychologically intolerable unless there is an overall cause and an overall purpose. It's this feeling which underlies a number of traditional 'proofs' for the existence of God, which don't in fact prove anything.

These two interpretations – religion as statements of fact, giving verifiable information, and religion as an expression of people's feelings, or ways or life, or moral codes – are probably too simple. The language religious people talk may do other jobs : it might be designed, for instance, to arouse certain feelings in other people, rather than just express the speakers' feelings. Some of it may be purely ritualistic, like saying 'Your excellency', or 'Great king, whose dominions stretch from . . .' It's often difficult to say, with any particular piece of religious talk, just what it is supposed to be doing. The first chapter of Genesis in the Bible, for instance, might be an attempt to give information, to say how the world came into being; or it might be an attempt to show you the world through a certain pair of spectacles – as glorious, as divine, marvellous, impressive, and so on. But if you keep these two general interpretations in mind, it will be easier to judge the passages that follow properly. When you look at them, you ought to ask, 'What sort of talk is this, and is it good *of its kind*?' For, as we have seen, different kinds of talk have to meet different standards.

Questions
1. 'Jesus was the Son of God'; 'Jesus was the son of Mary'. Are these the same kind of statement? If not, what's the difference?
2. 'If pretty little bluebirds fly above the rainbow, why, oh, why can't I?' (from the song 'Over the Rainbow' in the film *The Wizard of Oz*, sung by Judy Garland). Answer: 'Because you're too heavy, Judy.' Is it a proper answer? Is it a proper question?
3. Is religion just a matter of taste?
4. 'You believe in religion by faith, not reason.' Comment.
5. 'God always preserves the righteous.' Could you prove this to be true or false?
6. 'Religion is just a question of how you have been brought up.' Comment.
7. 'Psalms and hymns are just poetry.' Comment.

two

Moral Teaching

IN THIS chapter we shall try to say something about moral teaching, or, more exactly, about different *processes of persuasion* that can be adopted in the area of morality. In order to make our discussion as clear as possible, I shall use one particular example of a 'moral teacher' or a 'moral persuader' – the example of Jesus, as reported in the New Testament. This doesn't mean that I or anyone else has to be Christian (or anti-Christian); I use the example simply because it is likely to be familiar. Indeed, you may be able to see, during the course of this chapter, how in philosophy one can talk about morality, or about the way in which a particular person like Jesus does his teaching, without at all having to agree or disagree with any particular moral views that he puts forward.

We ought perhaps to start by feeling ourselves at a loss. There is a sort of gap, or vacuum of non-comprehension, in our approach to the New Testament and the words and actions of Jesus. Christians commonly believe that Jesus 'freed humanity from the law' – not so much the dead letter, but certainly the killing letter of the law – and introduced us to 'the spirit which giveth life'. We have moved, they say, from the list of moral rules to something else, to another way of looking at morality and hence another way of living.

But if we're asked to describe this different way of looking at morality, we find it curiously hard. We might reply that it's something to do with 'inner attitudes', or concepts like love and forgiveness; we might illustrate it by examples from Christian lives – the lives of the saints, for instance – and we might talk about 'the spirit of Christ working within us', and so on. But this is really not so much insufficient as irrelevant: because all we're really saying is that it isn't a morality based on rules and laws. But if it isn't like the Old Testament then what is it like? What is the logic of it? Just how does Jesus put over this morality? Then perhaps we say, 'Well, He produced parables and beatitudes and so on,' but even this isn't really an answer. For how do they work? The logic of a morality like the Ten Commandments is fairly clear, but the logic of Jesus' ethic isn't. And this ought to worry us, for quite a lot of reasons.

The basic reason why we're fogged is that we're bewitched by a certain dominating idea of what morality ought to be like and how it can be taught and argued about. Philosophers are just as bewitched as anybody else, hence the extreme dryness and implausibility of most examples in textbooks of moral philosophy. There's a sense in which we don't take Jesus' ethic *seriously*; Jesus' 'philosophy' doesn't find a place in the textbooks, even as illustrative material. We feel that what he says isn't anything to do with logic or philosophy; it's real life. In fact we have a very simple and naïve idea of what Jesus said and did as a moral teacher, roughly along these lines: (1) He was a shining example and went about doing good; (2) He laid down some moral ideals like love and forgiveness; (3) He laid down a few – to some people, distressingly few – rules about not doing this and that. Modern Christian textbooks tend to follow the same lines: they start by saying that things like love are good and things like pride are bad, and then they get down to rules about lying and gambling and drunkenness and (of course) sex. It's as if this were the only kind of moral teaching we could conceive.

To be a little more precise, our mistake is this; that we regard the model or classic case of moral teaching as the *rule* or *command*. Plenty of people, if asked how children learn their moral values, say that it's by their parents saying things like, 'It's wrong to steal', 'Don't lie', and so on. But even this isn't true. It's fairly obviously not true; indeed, if it were, we could predict that the most virtuous children would come from homes where the parents

it is a question of being reminded by rules or injunctions of what we really already know. Not much new experience, and certainly not much raw experience, is given to us if we are told not to steal or not to commit adultery. The words 'steal' and 'adultery' are governed by a set of familiar facts. We don't have to get the feel even of a new concept, in the sense that Jesus' use of 'love' represents a new concept, or in which a parable such as the Prodigal Son might illuminate the concept of forgiveness.

Between these poles fall a number of methods of presentation which it's not easy to categorize. Nearest to the raw experience of direct action I should place what we might call the imitation of action, that is, a story. The logic of parables is, roughly, that they act as microcosms or little worlds in themselves, in which pieces of the raw experience of life are assembled for a particular purpose and are driven home into our hearts by the author's skill in assembling them. They have the advantage over direct action in that the author can assemble the bits of life he wants, and hence fulfil his purpose more easily and less clumsily; they might be thought to lose in that the experience has to come through the medium of symbols and hence waters down the quality of directness, or rawness, that real-life experience has. A story about, or even a picture of, a leper is less direct than the actual sight of a leper, but equally it is more illuminating, because it can assemble more features -- and in so far as human beings have imagination it need not, in fact, be less direct in the sense of being less potent or effective.

We're accustomed to think sometimes that Jesus spoke in parables because he often spoke to 'simple folk' (peasants and so on) who could only understand if he talked about farmers and seed and vineyards, as if the real point could be perfectly well summarized in an indicative sentence; e.g. 'The point of the parable of the Good Samaritan is that you ought to help anyone in trouble.' But this is like thinking that Shakespeare can be translated without loss into prose, as if the lesson of *Macbeth* were 'Ambition doesn't pay', or of *Hamlet*, 'Don't be neurotic'. We regard indicative sentences and commands as important, and other forms of language as not really counting. It's as if the parables were like *Aesop's Fables*, with a moral at the end, stories for children, but the point of which adults can easily get without imaginatively absorbing the story. I don't think this is true even of Aesop, and certainly not of the parables.

Next to the category of parables come the category of teaching by images, but images of a less extended kind. These images might be used in various contexts, of which I can mention three:

(1) Rhetoric and insults, in which he uses an image to bring home the spiritual state of a person to him, to make him see himself for what he is; as for instance when he calls the Pharisees 'hypocrites' or 'whitewashed tombs'.

(2) Specific demands to people in particular states of mind, as when he tells the virtuous young man to go and sell all that he has. I count this as an image because, as in all these cases, he's presenting a sudden shock-picture, together with a touch of irony: 'One thing thou lackest: go, sell all thou hast . . .' – just one small thing!

(3) What I can only call squibs or paradoxes, in the sense that they're meant to disturb our thinking: as when he says, 'He that hateth not his father and his mother for my sake', and so on. This is a well-known technique, found also in Confucianism, Zen Buddhism and other religions.

In all these, Jesus shoots clear images at us in an attempt to disturb us. The images are clear because their significance is immediately comprehensible; we all know what hypocrites are and what hating one's parents is. It's the context in which he places them that disturbs us, and may change our point of view.

Lastly, near to the pole of rules and commandments but by no means right *at* the pole, is the erection of new concepts used without images. This is not so much a giving of new experience as an invitation to gain new experience via the use of the concepts. Thus the concepts of love, self-sacrifice, ministry and others, as used by Jesus, ask (as it were) to be learnt. We learn them by the kind of image-illustrations I've mentioned above, but the very existence of what is, in effect, a new language offers us a new slant on the world, a new way of looking at things. To learn the proper use of these terms, as in learning all languages, is to learn how to correlate the words with certain experiences. Of course with sense-experience this is easy, but with moral experience it's hard. This is why the terms are so vague in ordinary language. There is a word love, and perhaps after we've lived a bit we want to make a distinction between love and sex or infatuation, but we can only do this seriously if we are at least imaginatively aware of the difference between two states of mind. It's quite possible, however, to start with the words and then collect the experiences; indeed different words almost guide one into differentiation of experience : the psychological world of the Greeks, with their words *ero*, *philo*, *agapo* and *stergo* (all standing for different kinds of love), would have been very different from ours. If a man said, 'I love you' in Greek he'd have had to commit himself to a particular word, instead of leaving it vague as now. (For certain men who like to leave things vague this might be very awkward.) To try to learn the meaning of Christian terms is to seek for images and experience that will enable one to be sure of making the right distinctions in language.

Of course these concepts aren't wholly new : most of them are extensions of concepts we already have. It's this kind of extension which best illustrates the difference between the law and the spirit. It's here that work needs to be done. Suppose we produce a Christian concept like 'pure in heart' or 'chastity'. Now once we see that this isn't tied down to specific law-governed actions – as 'pure in heart' doesn't just mean not understanding vulgar words, nor 'chastity' just not sleeping with people – we're apt to say simply that it's 'the spirit of chastity' that counts, as if the new concept were somehow vaguer about it, precisely because we haven't worked hard enough at collecting experience : we haven't used our imaginations. I think a really well-developed conscience, or perhaps one should say imagination, would be able to tell without difficulty when this new concept of chastity was being properly

used and when it wasn't, and it would certainly cover far more
ground than just sex. Learning this sort of thing is a matter of
recognition, of understanding oneself, of being honest, patient and
careful with one's own feelings. In this context it seems to me that
any person, Christian or not, that doesn't take all forms of self-
knowledge seriously (or at least the forms of literature and
psychology), can't seriously be said to be trying to improve his
morality.

We're still accustomed, I believe, to make a very sharp distinction between two kinds of moral difficulties. First, there are
those cases when we know what's right but can't do it – cases of
weakness of will, where, 'I cannot do that which I would.' In these
cases Christians are apt to say that we see what's right but have to
ask Jesus' help to do it. Second, there are cases where we don't
know what's right, and then we have to work it out, or we have to
be given a rule or an ideal. But this distinction, if it exists at all, is
far more blurred than that. We ought rather to say (particularly
since Freud) that we don't really know what's right even in the
first case; we *don't see it right*. When I take another cigarette I
don't really see it as a cancer-bearing drug, not at the actual time.
We're under compulsions, and a compulsion is precisely a case of
not seeing ourselves and the situation clearly.

Hence if we were to try to justify, as opposed to merely describ-
ing, Jesus' moral teaching, we should do so not by asking whether
he propounded 'the right' rules or produced 'sound arguments' for
ideals, but by whether his presentation of words and images was
effective. By 'effective' we should mean, not just that it promoted
certain kinds of actions, for you can do that by hypnosis, brain-
washing or propaganda. We should want to know whether it was
illuminating, whether it showed us to ourselves; perhaps whether
– and this is what distinguishes it from propaganda – it was
liberating, and enlarged and strengthened the personality as
opposed to diminishing and restricting it; whether it gave us
more insight and hence more control. These criteria, which apply
in some sense to works of art and literature just as to moral
presentations, have the merit of covering the direct actions of

which I have spoken, as well as what we usually call 'moral arguments'.

So moving from the pole of direct action (the presentation of raw experience) to the imitation of action by parables, to teaching by less extended images, to the use of new concepts that invite the collection of new experience, we reach the other pole of rules and imperatives. It would be quite wrong to turn up our noses at these; they are, as it were, our staple diet, they keep us going. If we break them there must be something very wrong with our moral outlook indeed. But they can be used as a defence, and usually are, because to make moral progress by the use of imagination is very hard work and very painful. Experience hurts us, from the experience of being born onwards.

Questions
1. Name three different types of 'moral teaching', and explain how they work.
2. What sort of moral teaching do you think is most effective, and for what purpose?
3. Do we need moral rules, or just a well-developed imagination?
4. Do people ever do wrong deliberately, and knowing exactly what they're doing?
5. Do people always learn by experience? How does this sort of learning work? Is it automatic?
6. How far is sex a moral matter?
7. Is literature relevant to morality?

three

Works of Art

PEOPLE SPEND a lot of time talking about books and paintings and music, poetry and sculptures and buildings, the 'interior decoration' of their houses, and the kind of clothes they like to wear. Sometimes they just express their opinions: they say that they like a certain kind of pop music, or that they don't like a certain kind of wallpaper. But sometimes they *argue* about such things: one person tries to persuade another that a painting is a *good* painting, or that certain clothes are *ugly*, or that a book is *boring*. This kind of talk raises a lot of questions about how one ought to argue or think about such things. How can one tell whether a piece of music is good or bad? What sorts of reasons are there for liking or not liking it? Do the same sort of reasons apply to books and paintings? How about clothes – is it just a matter of what's in fashion, or are some clothes really beautiful and ugly?

The most important, and also the most difficult, question which can be raised here is the question of how one would define this sort of talk in general – whether one can put it into a particular category of its own. Thus there is a special kind of talk (and special kinds of reasons) we use when we're engaged in mathematics, another for science, another for morals, another for history, and so on. Is there a special kind of talk which we use for books, paintings, music, etc.? Philosophers in the past have usually supposed that there was, and have called it 'aesthetics', that is, a kind of talk that is about 'works of art'. But we need to look at this rather more closely.

Just what *is* a 'work of art'? This is harder to answer than we might think. We might start by saying, 'Well, works of art are things like books and buildings, etc.' But not all books and buildings are works of art. A Latin grammar or a cookery book isn't, nor is a pre-fab house or a garden shed. Now we might want to say, 'This is because Latin grammars and garden sheds aren't exciting, or beautiful; whereas good novels and cathedrals are exciting and beautiful, and so they count as works of art.' This is the view that what makes something a work of art is whether it has certain *qualities*, perhaps particularly whether it is beautiful.

But there are difficulties with this view :

(1) This doesn't distinguish works of art from ordinary natural objects. Girls can be beautiful, even if they're not wearing clothes or make-up, but they're not works of art. You can have a beautiful day, or a beautiful view from a mountain, but this isn't anything to do with art either. Birds sing beautifully, but this is by nature and not by art.

(2) Is it true, anyway, that works of art *all* have some particular quality like beauty? We might reasonably call a painting of lovely flowers, or a flattering portrait of some lovely woman beautiful. But suppose we have a painting of some horror scene (like Picasso's 'Guernica'), or a portrait where the artist has deliberately made the face look ugly? It seems odd to call that sort of thing 'beautiful'; we would more probably say that it was 'effective', or 'clever', or 'striking', or 'grim'.

(3) We have to allow for saying that there are *bad* works of art. I might write a sonnet, and it might not be beautiful (or interesting, or amusing, or anything of that kind), but surely it would still count as a work of art, even if it was a bad one.

Now we may be struck by the force of the word 'art', and the contrast with 'nature' (see (1) above); and hence we might say that one condition that a thing must satisfy, if it's to count as a work of art, is that somebody must have made it artificially; it can't just have occurred naturally. I'm not sure whether this is right or not. It certainly seems right, because we don't normally count majestic mountain scenes, or people, or the singing of birds as works of art. But suppose, just for the sake of example, that a bird suddenly sang a tune which got into the top twenty on the pop music charts, and everyone enjoyed it in just the same way as they enjoyed other pop records. Or suppose that a volcano erupted, and all the rock and molten lava fell down in such a way that it made a marvellous building or piece of sculpture. Would we call such cases 'works of art' or not?

This is one of those cases in philosophy where perhaps it doesn't matter very much whether we jump one way or the other. What's happened is that we have two possible things in mind, two criteria for the phrase 'work of art'. One is the criterion that it has to be *artificially made* (by human beings); the other is that it can be *looked at*, or *reacted to*, in a certain kind of way (by human beings). We may, if we like, insist on the first criterion as being necessary. But the second criterion is also important, as we shall see.

A work of art can't just be *anything* made by human beings. We saw this from the examples of a Latin grammar and a garden shed. Why aren't these works of art? We might now want to say, 'Because they're not intended as such; they're meant to be practical things, not the sort of things which people are going to judge or enjoy "aesthetically", or call beautiful or ugly. A good Latin grammar is one which is clear, informative, accurate, easy to read and look up words in, and so on; but a good novel or a good play has got to be exciting, interesting, amusing, dramatic, etc. – it doesn't matter whether it's "accurate" or "informative".' There is an important truth here; that when we judge things as works of art, rather than for practical purposes, we use different words and have different reasons in mind. It's one thing to judge a car or an aeroplane from the practical point of view – does it go fast, is it economical on petrol, does it need a lot of repairs? – and quite another to judge it as a work of art – is it painted in an attractive colour, does it *look* fast, is it styled gracefully?

But we still haven't got it quite right. It's true that very often, perhaps usually, people intend the works of art they make to be such. That is, they say to themselves, 'I'm going to try to make something attractive, beautiful, amusing, etc., and not just something that works well.' But this doesn't always happen. Sometimes people have made things for quite different purposes – for the purposes of religion, or practical purposes – and yet what they made were very fine works of art. For instance, the Romans built the Pont du Gard in Provence for quite down-to-earth purposes: they wanted an aqueduct to carry water. Similarly some Victorian engineers, like Brunel, built bridges simply to carry traffic, but quite a lot of people think that what they built are impressive works of art. So the *intentions* of the person who made the thing aren't necessarily important. It seems to be rather a matter of the *way in which we look* at what's made.

This is perhaps one reason why many modern works of art are not so much carefully-contrived objects, as they were in the past, but rather natural objects presented *as* works of art, or else objects made for practical purposes presented as works of art. Thus an art exhibition might contain some curiously-shaped stones or bits of wood from the sea-shore, things just found (*objets trouvés*) rather than made; or quite practical things like lamp-posts and drain covers. Similarly 'concrete music' is often a series of natural noises (squeaks, bangs, etc.) rather than the artificial noises produced by using the normal notes of music in the octave. And when we think of such cases as making a garden, making a chair, painting a house or designing a motorway, we can see how blurred is the borderline between 'works of art' and other things.

Nevertheless the borderline is there; the difference depends on the way in which we look at, or read, or listen to something. But what is this way? We have seen that it is a way of approaching things which causes us to use some words ('exciting', 'beautiful', etc.) and not others ('useful', 'cheap', etc.); but this isn't good enough. For we use the former words about natural objects also: holidays can be exciting and the weather beautiful. What's the difference between a beautiful girl and a beautiful statue, between an exciting holiday and an exciting story, between a horrifying death on the roads and a horror film?

Whatever the difference is, it is an important and interesting one. For it should strike us that, when we apply words like 'sad', 'horrifying', 'grim', etc., to works of art, we don't at all imply that the works of art are *unpleasant* or to be avoided. People don't enjoy being horrified in real life, but they do enjoy horror films. People avoid sad experiences in real life, but flock to see 'sad' plays or 'sad' films. Indeed this difference suggests that we ought to put the words into inverted commas, as I have just put 'sad', when they are used about works of art. We might be tempted to say that 'sad' music isn't really sad, since people obviously enjoy it and go away feeling pleased.

It is fairly obvious that the difference comes about because we look on works of art as, in a very broad sense, *imitations* of what we experience in our ordinary lives. We know that the horrific scenes in a horror film 'aren't real'; they are only 'play'. The crucial step towards art is taken when a person stops doing things naturally, and begins imitating, or representing, or making a play out of his real-life feelings and experiences. He has to do this by using *conventions* or symbols. For instance, if I am angry, I might snarl and shake my fist; somebody watching me might feel frightened and dislike it. But if I make a mime out of it, and (as it were) go through the motions of being angry, snarling and shaking my fist as conventional gestures, then this is an elementary form of art or drama.

What is curious about this imitative or 'artificial' (as opposed to natural) behaviour is that human beings *enjoy* it. Psychologists can tell us a lot about why it is that children enjoy playing for its own sake, whether dogs and cats do too, why worms and ants don't play, and so on, but this belongs to another subject. What we need to note here is that not all the imitative or 'artificial' behaviour of human beings is enjoyable in this way. Thus, I might shake my fist not as a piece of mime or drama, but perhaps to warn somebody that I was angry with him, or in order to show the gods that I thought they were being unjust. In the same way we can use words and paintings not only as works of art (in the form of poems and pictures), but also to give instructions, make maps, teach biology and do hundreds of other quite practical things. When we do this, we don't enjoy or 'appreciate' the words and paintings *for their own sake*; we use them, as means to gain a particular end (making something clear, giving a direction, teaching a subject).

So the striking thing about 'works of art' is that they're enjoyed or appreciated or valued for their own sake; they're not supposed to be *useful*. But at the same time, they're not enjoyed in the same way that we enjoy eating chocolate, or looking at a beautiful view, or hearing birds sing: they're enjoyed as imitations, or as forms of play, or as representations. Hence there is a close connection between works of art and our feelings and emotions as human beings: works of art, in a sense, represent or imitate our feelings. The connection between (say) eating chocolate and our feelings is quite different: here it's just that chocolate satisfies us or gives us pleasure. The chocolate doesn't in any way represent or symbolize our feelings, it just satisfies them. But a sonnet about love, or a majestic symphony, or a catchy pop tune, or a dramatic painting, or the soaring spire of a cathedral, doesn't *just* give us pleasure: these things are somehow in themselves representations of our feelings, and they give us the kind of pleasure that human beings characteristically get from such representations. The difference is that between a child having a good meal on the one hand, and a child making up a simple game on the other: he enjoys both, but in different ways.

But we must be careful about saying that works of art 'imitate' or 'represent'. Suppose (1) we draw an ordinary map, as accurately as we know how, in order to show travellers which way to go. It would 'represent' the actual countryside accurately, and might be said to 'tell the truth' about where the hills, valleys, rivers and towns were. Now suppose (2) we draw a sort of imaginary map, like some maps in the Middle Ages, or like a map of some non-existent country such as Ruritania: we put pictures of dragons and dolphins in it, and little cherubs with puffed cheeks to show which way the winds blow. (1) isn't a work of art; (2) is.

(2) doesn't represent any *actual facts* about the world, or tell the *truth* about any country; rather, it *symbolizes* certain human feelings, or represents them in a concrete form – excitement and danger is symbolized by dragons, and so on. Here it's the merits of the *symbols themselves* which count : the dragon can be well or badly drawn, the cherubs can look pretty or ugly, the dolphins in the sea can seem exciting or boring. In (1), however, it doesn't matter much what signs you use to mark a hill, or valley, or town, so long as the signs are clear and tell you accurately where things are.

This distinction between *signs* and *symbols* is a useful one for our purposes. Words used in prose, for practical purposes, are just signs; they are purely conventional, and we judge their merits by whether they make the author's meaning clear and whether they are true. But words used in poetry are important in themselves; they are symbols of the author's feelings, or of the feelings of his readers. Whether the poem is any good or not depends on whether the symbols do this job well; that is, the job of evoking and representing feelings. Different symbols carry different emotional significance in themselves. But whether a practical handbook or textbook is any good or not depends simply on whether the signs (words) are clear and correctly used. This is why you can't translate a poem into another language without losing a great deal of its original merit, whereas a textbook may be just as good in any language.

Poems and plays and novels, then, and still more obviously paintings and buildings and sculptures and music, don't *tell the truth*; whereas textbooks and photographs and tape-recordings can tell the truth, or state facts. Yet because of their important connection with human feelings, works of art are not *just* amusing, or pleasurable, or exciting. As well as giving us pleasure (like chocolates or wine), they also influence us. We may even say that they *teach* us, though 'teach' here won't mean anything like telling us facts. What they do is more like evoking our feelings, and then putting them in order, so that, at the end, we feel not just that we have enjoyed ourselves, but that we have had something *done* to us – that our emotions are now in a more satisfactory state.

It is very hard to describe exactly what happens here. But one obvious case is when we watch a good play or read a good novel. Some plays or novels may excite or interest us, but be bad as works of art. For instance, many Westerns, or thrillers, or love stories really only represent very simple or childish feelings : there are 'good guys' and 'bad guys', virtue is rewarded, the heroine marries the hero in the end, and so on. We may get the same sort of pleasure out of these as we get out of having a drink or eating chocolate, but somehow we don't *learn* anything. In a good play or a good novel – that is, something that is good *as* a play or *as* a novel, and not just something which is pleasant as a bit of escapism, or to pass an idle moment in the train – we may be moved to feel things that we haven't felt before, to consider our fee. ngs, and to reorganize them. We become more perceptive about the motives of the characters in the story or the play; perhaps they can't be divided into 'good guys' and 'bad guys' quite so simply, but rather they're partly good and partly bad. Or we may not worry so much about whether they are 'good' or 'bad', but just understand how they feel. A Shakespearean hero, like Hamlet or Macbeth or Othello, isn't a hero in the same sense that a Western hero is. Hamlet is more interesting because he's more complicated, and *more like ourselves*.

When we argue about works of art, then, we're not arguing just about what we enjoy or don't enjoy. This is to treat works of art as if they were entirely matters of taste (like whether we prefer milk chocolate or plain chocolate). We argue about whether we ought to enjoy them, whether they're good as works of art. Thus a very young child will only enjoy simple-minded comics, or fairy stories, but we think that he ought to grow up to enjoy – 'appreciate', if you like – stories that have more to do with people as they really are. What are commonly accepted as 'great' artists – Shakespeare, Beethoven, Michelangelo, etc. – are only great because they really do express and represent human feelings in the most forceful and effective way.

It is not always easy to appreciate or enjoy great artists, for two reasons. First, they may write (or paint, or compose, or whatever) in a style or manner which is unfamiliar to us today. Thus some old-fashioned people are still not used to those modern paintings which (as they say) 'don't look like what they're supposed to be'; and some people can't get used to the rhythms and guitar-noises and so forth that are characteristic of some pop music. One has first to get used to the style, to 'learn the language' (so to speak) of the artist. This is largely just a matter of practice, but it can be accelerated by paying deliberate attention to what the artist does : to the metre of poems, the plots of novels, the harmonies of a particular composer, and so on.

The other reason has to do with our own feelings. Thus it may be that a person finds it hard to face his own feelings of pity, horror, anxiety, etc., when these are evoked by some tragic drama; or it may be that he is too disturbed by the *complexity* of the motives of some character in a novel for him to appreciate the novel. If a person can't stand the thought of an 'unhappy ending', or feels lost without some superman hero who wins all the fights and always does the right thing, then he is unlikely to appreciate a good deal of literature. Of course this reason is very closely connected with the first reason. It may be difficult for a person to familiarize himself with the style of a writer or artist, to 'learn his language', partly *because* the 'language' is new or frightening in some way. Old-fashioned people who wish to 'get used to modern art' have to make a psychological effort, not just a study of Picasso's techniques.

Arguments about works of art are not profitable unless they attempt to deal with one or both of these two obstacles to appreciation. We may, indeed, profitably argue about (say) the date of a Shakespearean play, or the intentions of a poet in writing a poem, or the kind of instruments used in a pop group; or we may argue – as we have been doing – about what it means to call something 'a work of art'. But this isn't arguing about works of art *as such*; the date of a play isn't in itself relevant to the play as a work of art. The only point in talking about works of art, if our object is to increase our appreciation and enjoyment of them, is to demolish or reduce the obstacles to that appreciation and enjoyment.

In practice we wouldn't exactly *argue* about a piece of music or a poem or a book. We would rather try to say helpful things, in conjunction with a person's listening to the music or reading the poem or book. Perhaps while he listens we might say, 'Isn't it wonderful how the bass guitar comes in here, listen . . .'; or when he's read the book, 'Hasn't the author caught the mood and despair just perfectly, do you remember the passage where . . .' We can helpfully do this before the person's experience of the work of art, or during it, or after it. But in all cases what we're trying to do is to *guide his attention*. Sometimes it may help if he can take something on trust from us: we might say, 'Now this bit of music is tremendously power and majestic: you may not see it at first, but give yourself time – play the record four or five times – and you'll come to realize it later.' Critics of literature, art and music do many things, but this should be their chief job. It is also a job which is well worth doing for oneself, for by trying to express clearly just what it is that one enjoys about a work of art, one usually comes to appreciate it more.

Questions
1. Can a carpet be a work of art? A knife? A dog?
2. What's the difference between a painting and a photograph?
3. Are all works of art beautiful?
4. 'Art for art's sake.' What could this mean?
5. Novels are about people; so are textbooks of psychology and history. What's the difference?
6. Do poems tell the truth?
7. 'Pop music is better than classical.' Could you show this to be true or false?

II
CONCEPTS IN
POLITICS

four

Democracy

DEMOCRACY IS something that almost everybody in this society prizes highly. It is something we're proud of; something which we rather like to show off to other less fortunate countries. We contrast it favourably with Communism, Fascism, tyranny, dictatorship, and other forms of government. We speak freely of certain actions as 'undemocratic'; we call ourselves one of the great 'western democracies'. If we value this thing so highly, it is well to be clear about what precisely it is that we value, and this will lead us to consider whether or not we're wise in valuing it. For since nearly all questions about our form of government, our constitution, and our political behaviour involve the value of democracy, it is plain that we shan't get far in answering such questions without considering it.

In this country we're accustomed to think of democracy as what may be called 'parliamentary democracy'. The most important feature of democracy, as it appears to us, is the right to elect our own national parliament. Every five years, or sometimes at shorter intervals, we exercise this right by voting for the candidates in our parliamentary constituency; those elected by the majority vote become our leaders in a very real sense. Legally, parliament is the sovereign body of England, and not the people of England; the people exercise sovereign rights only at election times. The parliament has sovereign powers which we are bound to obey; our only direct control over it is a long-term control, by our election of its members.

All this is obvious enough; but think how narrow this conception of democracy is. Consider the actual derivation of the word.

The Greek 'democratia', from which our 'democracy' derives, means 'control by the demos'. And though 'demos' means 'the people', the Greeks at least didn't always use the word as we sometimes use 'the people'. To them it often meant 'the common people', almost 'the lower classes', 'the masses', or what a Communist would call 'the proletariat', meaning roughly 'the working classes'. In this use, 'the people' contrasts with any other class of individuals within a state : a few aristocrats, a few rich men, a king, or tyrant, or dictator, or any minority class in the society. If this class, rather than 'the people', hold most or all of the power in the state, then the state is not to be called a democracy : we call it an oligarchy (government of the few), a plutocracy (government of the rich), a tyranny, and so on.

It's worth noticing that 'democracy' in this sense does not always coincide with 'democracy' in our more usual modern sense of 'government by a majority of the adult members of a community'. By 'the people' we usually mean simply all the adult members of our society, without special reference to the 'lower classes' or 'the masses'. In ancient Athens, for instance, a very large proportion of the adults were slaves, and had no vote; yet the Athenians still called themselves a democracy, because the chief power was still in the hands of the lower classes, and not in the hands of oligarchs, tyrants, or any minority class. Similarly, I think we in England would have called ourselves a democracy, even before we had allowed women to vote; though we should at that time have denied the vote to about half the adult members of our society. Generally speaking, however, we needn't attach too much importance to this distinction. For the majority of adult members of almost any society consists of the 'lower classes', that is, to make a very rough attempt to explain a phrase whose meaning is generally understood, salaried workers in the lower income groups, factory workers, farm labourers, peasants, and so forth.

Nevertheless, the distinction is important in one respect. It makes us realize that unless the 'lower classes' do actually hold most of the political power, we are not entitled to call any society a democracy in either sense. For if they don't hold most of the power, then most of the power is held by a minority group, since the 'lower classes' are in the vast majority. It makes an important difference, I think, to face ourselves with the question, not, 'Is our constitution democratic?' but more realistically and in more concrete terms, 'Do the lower classes hold most of the political power in England?' If we look at this question honestly, it may well occur to some of us even to question the value of democracy. One can well imagine somebody wanting what he might call a democratic constitution, but not wanting the lower classes to exercise most of the political power. Yet if he said this, he would plainly be using the phrase 'democratic constitution' in a narrow sense. He would mean, perhaps, only that the lower classes should exercise some sort of long-range control, as at parliamentary elections; or that their wishes and views should be consulted and taken notice of; or, at least, that the ruling classes should not do anything which the lower classes would be violently opposed to. This may indeed be a sensible view, but it seems unfair to use the word 'democracy' to support it, since the system of political control it proposes would in fact be a modified and perhaps disguised oligarchy.

There's very little doubt that England is not yet a democratic country in the full sense; political control is not exercised by a majority of people, but by a minority. This is true despite the highly important modifications that have been gradually introduced into a society which two hundred years ago was in no sense a democracy. In theory, perhaps the most important of these modifications is the right to vote for parliamentary candidates every five years, and hence to exercise indirect and long-range control over the opinions of our rulers. But in practice, the attention which is paid to the will of the people as a whole by their rulers is of more real importance. Parliament knows that it can't do entirely as it likes. It may, and frequently does, pass measures which are not in accordance with the will of the people, but at least it knows that the people won't tolerate everything. The majority's will acts in effect as a kind of touchstone, a test which every parliamentary measure must pass. If it fails to pass the test, it's not necessarily damned, but an important point is chalked up against it.

In so far as this society is democratic, it is chiefly so in a negative way; that is, as I've said, the will of the people acts as a sort of veto to any outrageously unpopular measures. It is also true that when there is an organized, vocal and overwhelming body of public opinion in favour of a particular measure, that measure, or something like it, usually gets carried sooner or later; the people do possess some degree of positive control. With all these allowances, however, Britain still falls short of full democracy. For it is not enough for democracy that government should be *according* to the will of the people. If that were the whole significance of the word, the country could be governed by a benevolent despot or a well-intentioned oligarchy. Democracy implies that the *power* is in the hands of the people, that the people exercise a control over political affairs which, whether direct or indirect, is still real power. And it is here, I think, that our democratic system falls short.

The actual political power in England is for the most part distributed throughout various bodies over which the people as a whole have remarkably little control. We might list here bodies like the House of Commons, the House of Lords, the Civil Service, the local County and Borough Authorities, the Press, and the criminal and civil law courts. Over some of these bodies the people exercise an indirect control by means of election, as with the House of Commons and the local authorities; over others of them, such as the Press, they exercise an indirect economic control, since newspapers and magazines have to sell in order to survive; and over others, such as the House of Lords, the Civil Service and the law courts, their control is so indirect as to be virtually non-existent. It's true that, in theory, the House of Commons holds the supreme power, and can control all other bodies; and it's true that this House is elected by the people – or by as many of the people as consider it worth their while to vote at general and by-elections. But in fact the absence of any direct control over political events and decisions makes this indirect control largely ineffective. Most people, once every five years, are presented with the opportunity of voting for one out of a number of candidates (often only two), of whose views, disposition, intelligence and ability they can know very little; and what they do know affects only certain topics, such as our economic organization, which are the chief concern of the political parties of which the candidates are members. In local elections, similarly, the candidates are often almost as remote, and few people talk or think as if they had any real stake in the doings of the Mayor and Councillors, the local education authority, and so forth.

Part of the trouble is undoubtedly that those who rule – those who are members of the bodies who have real political control – are sharply divided from those who elect them. They may be divided by social class, by wealth, or by many other differences (they may just lead different sorts of lives and never mix with the others, for instance). Cases where a 'man of the people' – somebody really poor, and without much education – is elected occur, but they're rare. It is thus difficult for the people to do very much more than trust to one particular candidate, and allow him to carry on with the job. This system may, indeed, be a better one than true democracy, but it hardly places any real political control in the hands of the general public. It's not generally felt that the ordinary citizen can, by word or action, do anything which will really *change* the situation; the control is so indirect, and the consequent inertia and apathy so great, that a great many people are content to be governed rather than to govern. We may argue and discuss, but we don't feel that our arguments and discussions have any real political effect.

Further, our system is not such that the people can intervene over important questions of the moment. It's not part of the British tradition to have frequent referenda, or to find out by other means what the views of the people actually are. Consider questions like capital punishment, the disestablishment of the Church of England, religious education, the divorce laws, British colonies, expenditure of education, taxation, and a host of others. Does anybody really know what the majority view on these questions is? I doubt it. Does any member of those bodies who have political power actually want to know? I suspect very few. Would the governing bodies, if the majority opinion were known to tend in one direction, actually pass measures to put this opinion into practice? Not necessarily. For that isn't our way; we prefer, in fact, not to go by public opinion, but to count public opinion simply as one factor in government – and not by any means the most important one.

How far should we agree to this situation? We must admit, on the one hand, that in a country of any size or complexity, a great deal of control exercised by the people has to be indirect, if the system of government is not to become unstable and cumbersome. It's not possible, for instance, for a majority of the citizens living in England to decide every move in our foreign policy in detail; and it would be unwise to have elections so frequently that a stable and consistent foreign policy became impossible, owing to a continuous change of government or of the members of the House of Commons. Again, we must also admit that it is wise to trust to experts where these are available. The majority of citizens couldn't balance a budget, or produce competent and effective measures for the prevention of disease; this would be correctly left to Treasury experts and medical authorities. Precisely how far experts are available is always a difficult question; balancing a budget is a clear case where one must trust financial experts, but what about education? How far, and in what cases, are we to trust the educational authorities and experts, as opposed to our individual judgement? Everything depends, of course, on how far the experts can produce a consistent record of competent judgement; how far they can prove themselves right, and prove their knowledge superior to our own. Even then, of course, we've got to ensure that they are unbiased and acting in our best interests: they must be working to the ends which we ourselves desire, even though we may accept their judgement about how best to attain those ends – just as we must have faith that the doctor is trying to cure us, if we're to accept his expert advice on how the cure is to be achieved.

On the other hand, it's plain that the situation is far from ideal, that is, if we approve of democracy. For the control exercised by the people is far less than it could be. Now, although 'democratic' in almost all societies is a word of praise, and although it is generally supposed that the more democratic a country is the better, I feel that some of the considerations mentioned above may make many of us think twice before giving our unqualified support to democracy. This is particularly true if we understand 'democracy' as a system of government in which the 'lower classes' hold the bulk of power. Do we really approve of such a system? Do we really want our country run by factory workers, artisans, farm labourers, shop assistants, and so forth? More specifically, is it really our desire that these people should exercise direct and effective political power, or do we desire rather that they should stay in the political background, their role being limited to that of acting as a check to tyranny or a discouragement to despotism? Stated in this form, these questions might produce a considerable division of opinion amongst us. For that reason, it is important that we should first investigate our belief in the value of democracy.

The stock argument for democracy is a negative one: the argument that one can only prevent tyranny, totalitarianism, dictatorship and the misuse of power by individuals for their own ends, by granting the people enough political power to prevent such misuse. This is a good argument; but it is an argument, not so much for a *democratic* society – a society in which the people actually run the country – as for a *free* or *liberal* society – a society in which the people are not oppressed by a tyrant, in which different opinions and different types of behaviour can flourish without being suppressed by a dictatorial government. The argument, so to speak, seems to make the best of a bad job; it claims no virtue in the people running the country, but it points out (correctly) the dangers of oppression and selfishness on the part of the government. If this were the only argument for democracy, we could be quite content with the present state of affairs in this country. For to prevent oppression it is only necessary that the people should act as a check to tyranny; it is not necessary that they should take an active political part in our society.

There are, however, other arguments which support democracy in the true sense, arguments rarely mentioned, but which seem to me of the highest importance. Four of these are worth stating briefly :

(1) Although we may legitimately trust experts in certain fields, there are other questions where we have no expert guidance, and in trying to answer these questions, it's not at all obvious that one man's opinions are worth very much more than another's. Questions like : 'Should we hang murderers?', 'Should we tax the rich to pay for the needs of the poor?', 'Should divorce be made easier?', and 'Ought children to stay on at school until they are 17 years old?' aren't the sort of questions to which definite answers can be given by experts. In fact, there are no genuine experts to give such answers. And since ordinary people form the society in which these decisions are going to be made – since ordinary people will suffer or benefit from them – it is reasonable to suppose that they should have the chance to make them, not merely by electing people who (we hope) will represent their opinions accurately, but by ensuring that their opinions are given direct effect.

(2) Even on matters where we have expert guidance, the opinions of those who are affected by political decisions are always of value. An expert may tell us what is good for us, but unless he knows us very well indeed, his judgement is likely to be at fault. Even if he's right, what is good for us may not be what we want, and the dangers of giving people what is supposed to be good for them when they do not want it are obvious. In the comparatively short run, only those who are, as it were, at the receiving end of political decisions can judge effectively. Public opinion, therefore, must exercise a positive effect; it must be organized, and vocal, for only on the basis of such opinion can the correct decisions be made.

(3) A more important argument, in my view, is that it is psychologically desirable that people should control their own destiny and their own affairs. If they don't, we may expect (as we do indeed find) inertia, apathy, and a loss of that sense of responsibility and enthusiasm which alone can keep a society living and healthy. If our lives are organized for us, whether by a bureaucracy, a dictator, an oligarchy, or a dead weight of tradition, we can't be expected to take much interest in them. We shall be unable to feel that we have much stake in our society, to take an interest and a pride in it, to strive our hardest to improve its good points and root out its deficiencies. This is simply a psychological fact. If people have control, then they have interest and incentive; if they do not, they become resentful, irresponsible, and inert. Every man, to the best of his ability, should take an interest in, and assume some measure of responsibility for, his own life and the lives of his neighbours. He should strive for means to improve the lot of others, to remedy abuses, to achieve new objectives. And he can't do this if his role is a purely negative one. We need, not merely a stable society, but a healthy and growing one. We need, not only that people should benefit by the government of others, but that they should play an active part in benefiting others by their government. People are not slow to serve their community, if only they are given the chance. In time of war or serious crisis, when the issues can be made real and important to them, we see how readily and with what enthusiasm (and even heroism) our citizens lend their weight to the communal purpose. We desperately need some methods by which, when the crisis is past, ordinary people can serve their neighbours in the same spirit.

(4) Another disastrous consequence of the people's failure to exercise political control is that society inevitably becomes divided into two groups : those who rule, and those who are ruled. The dividing line between these groups may be blurred, and a great many people may be on the border-line, yet the distinction is a real one. 'The ruling classes' is not an entirely

empty phrase. The danger of the distinction is that it militates against those feelings of equality and independence that are necessary for a healthy and self-confident society. The rulers tend to become arrogant and complacent, while the ruled tend to become insecure, to feel inferior, and to lack confidence. This inferiority on the part of the ruled may, and often does, express itself in unnecessary aggressiveness and resentment; feeling that they do not have as much power as the ruling classes, they set out to prove to themselves and to others that their feeling is false. Symptoms of this are not hard to find, even in our own society (consider some strikes). Invariably, when this happens, class-consciousness survives, and there's often a cold war between the various classes, though in many societies this never develops into a shooting war. Equality and fraternity are out of the question, and even liberty suffers as a result, for the ruled tend to imagine (not always unjustly) that they are being imposed on by the rulers. For this reason it is essential that the people as a whole, not merely a section of society, should co-operate on an equal footing in political action. For most people, a negative role – which amounts virtually to the right of veto – is not a sufficient guarantee of independence and power. That is why no despotism or minority rule, however benevolent, can ever be really satisfactory.

Questions
1. In some countries women are not allowed to vote. Are these countries democratic?
2. In what sense does the ordinary British citizen have political *power*?
3. How can we distinguish between questions for experts and questions where one man's opinion is as good as another's?
4. Which of the four arguments for democracy given above (pp. 54–6) do you think the most important, and why?
5. Could you have a totalitarian or tyrannical democracy?

6. Are any of the arguments for democracy mentioned above relevant to settling the question of who should be allowed the vote? How about those aged 16–21, or criminals, or foreign immigrants?
7. What are the best arguments *against* democracy?

five

Law-making and Freedom

THE CHIEF problem in political theory has always been to find a general criterion of law-making. In the past it has been variously believed that the state is entitled to pass laws which the tribal elders approve, which are in line with the holy scriptures, which the Party thinks good, which 'every decent chap' would subscribe to, and so on. This has been found to lead to oppression and tyranny; to avoid these, most sophisticated people today subscribe to the liberal theory of law-making. This theory states, roughly, that no State should pass a law restricting freedom of individual action (actually, all laws by definition restrict), except in order to prevent people from restricting the freedom of others. More briefly : the State should only interfere to stop people interfering with each other. In the Western world this is perhaps the most popular, almost the official, basis of government. What I shall try to show here is that, unless it's radically reinterpreted, this theory is as useless, and can be as tyrannical, as any other theory.

First, let's be clear that if the theory is to be at all effective as a defence against oppression, it must not rely upon *majority opinion*, since majorities can be as oppressive as any other form of government. A white majority might oppress a black minority, a heterosexual majority oppress a homosexual minority, and so forth. The question of what is to count as 'interference' or 'a restriction upon freedom' must not be referred to majority opinion.

But then it seems impossible to make the concept of interference both effective and acceptable. We can make it effective – that is, sufficiently clearly-defined to operate as an effective criterion – by attaching it to some other criterion : thus, we could say that 'every decent chap' would regard sexual assault as interference, or that 'every right-thinking citizen' is interfered with by coloured people sharing the same restaurants, and add that what these people count as interference should be taken as really such, for purposes of government. But then this isn't acceptable, since we have opened the doors to tyranny again. On the other hand, we can make the criterion acceptable by refusing to attach it to what a partisan group of people think, or to any other criterion, but then it's got no teeth and is ineffective; we can hardly say what counts as interference and what does not.

This last point can be brought out by three examples :

(1) *Borderline cases.* There are plenty of these. I play my wireless loud enough to do justice to Beethoven or Wagner, but too loud to do justice to my neighbours. I walk around with no clothes, which is nice for me but nasty for the 'respectable' Mrs Grundy. I live in a caravan which saves me rent, but the snobbish people on the housing estate say it 'lowers the tone' of the area. In all these cases I have a desire and my neighbours have desires, and one of the two has to lose, but the concept of interference doesn't tell us which. If I turn off my radio so as not to interfere with my neighbour's peace and quiet, well; but then they are interfering with my music. Either I interfere with Mrs Grundy's peace of mind, or else she exercises tyranny over how I dress. Either I force my neighbours to 'lower the tone', or they force me to pay more rent. Of course these are not major problems, and no doubt compromises can be reached in practice. But what worries us is that the notion of interference seems to be useless.

(2) *Obscure cases.* These are also numerous. They are cases where we just don't know whether things would 'interfere' with society or not. It's curious that liberal, 'progressive' or 'enlightened' people who go to immense lengths not to harm any piece of ritual, convention, or custom in primitive peoples, on the grounds that we ought to know far more anthropology

before we start tampering, go quite wild when advocating changes in our own society. It may be, as many people hope and believe, that permitting adult homosexuality would not affect our society adversely; but then it may not be. It's reasonably plain that our society, and perhaps some people's passion for hard work and technology, is somehow bound up with sexual repression, and nobody can say whether a more liberal morality would not shake it to its foundations. This might be good or bad, but to say that adult homosexuality does not interfere with other people *may* be just naïve. It restricts the concept of interference to an absurdly small size: that is, to those cases where we can see with absolute clarity what the results of our actions are.

(3) *Lunatic cases.* Even supposing we said, 'Well, permitting homosexuality might shake society, but there's no real evidence of this, so let's allow homosexuals to enjoy their freedom anyway', we still have to face the large body of people whose desire is not to allow homosexuals their freedom. If we allow it, the desire of these people is thwarted; it is now they who are interfered with. If this sounds lunatic, there are plenty of similar cases. We have to appreciate that a really fanatical segregationist is interfered with by the presence of Negroes, an out-and-out Nazi by the presence of Jews, and an extreme puritan (and many people are a bit prejudiced here) at seeing people making love in public. One can even imagine a person who frothed at the mouth and fell down in fits whenever he saw someone with red hair. Here again the concept of interference isn't much use.

Perhaps our instinctive, common-sense reaction to such doubts is something like this : 'Come, we all really know what's interference and what isn't. If I murder someone or steal from him, that's interference; if I stand before him with red hair or no clothes or a black skin, that isn't; he can always look the other way if he doesn't like it. There may be borderline cases, but the very existence of a borderline shows that the concepts of interference and non-interference do occupy different areas. There may be obscure cases, but we shall just have to muddle through till we know more sociology. And as for the lunatic cases, well, they *are* lunatic. People who have fits when they see red hair need psychiatric treatment; we cannot consider them as normal citizens when we are thinking of making laws.'

Now of course it's true that, *in any one social group*, there are fairly clear concepts of interference and non-interference, just as there's a fairly clear distinction between which bits of a man's life are private and which are public. If, within that group, they choose to have a liberal theory of law-making, well and good. But their concepts of interference and of what is 'liberal' will be defined by the conventions and customs of that group. It may be what 'the ordinary citizen', or 'the decent chap', counts as interference, rather than what God is supposed to have said, or what is in the interests of the Party, and of course this *sounds* more liberal. But it isn't necessarily. The ordinary citizen may have the most appalling prejudices. Most do.

If the concept of interference is to cut any ice, in other words, it seems that it must depend on prejudice (in the strict sense of the word, i.e. a previous judgement) about what desires are to count as legitimate and what as illegitimate. And this seems to throw the whole thing back into the melting-pot. Thus, most societies don't like murder and theft; so they say that murderers interfere with the freedom of their victims, not that law-protected victims interfere with the desires of their murderers. But one could, rationally if not fashionably, prefer to live in a more competitive or piratical society, admiring the Homeric hero who was 'extremely skilful in stealing and oath-breaking'.

If this were accepted, we should at least have gained one thing: the recognition that there is no absolute decision to be made about what interferes and what does not, so that in one sense neither party in a conflict of desires is right or wrong. At present, for instance, one side will say that sharing restaurants with Negroes does interfere with their own freedom, and the other side will say, 'Don't be silly, it doesn't really interfere at all'. What we want is

rather the recognition that to *feel* interfered with by this, or anything else, is politically a *pity*, or a weakness – perhaps psychologically a weakness also. No doubt it's also politically a pity or a
weakness for Negroes to have to fulfil their desires by demanding
integration. But we could then go on to consider how central to
the concept of a human being, or human existence, various types
of feelings and activities were; and we might reach some general
agreement on this. Thus, although (to make things easier politically) perhaps I ought not to mind losing my life, health and
property, it is probably going to be more difficult to teach me this
than to teach my neighbour to refrain from murder, assault and
theft.

What we ought to be suspicious about, and what this rather
vague reconstruction of the liberal theory is supposed to avoid
(along with avoiding rigidity in the concept of interference), is the
notion that some desires are morally right and others reprehensible.
For politics, at least, the matter is simply one of convenience, and
if we can shelve not only the idea that we know what is good for
people, but also the idea that we know what 'really' interferes
with them, agreement would be more rapid. There are, after all,
certain laws which (so long as human beings remain human) we
must have. It would be difficult, logically as well as in practice, to
conceive of a society where any kind of killing, stealing and lying
was allowed to any degree whatsoever; these are central to the
concepts of human communication and coexistence. How far we
can persuade people out of other things which are often thought
to be as central as these is a matter for psychologists. It would be
a fair bet, for instance, that we shall learn to accept homosexuals
in a fairly short time (if indeed we haven't already), but that it
will take us a much longer time to regard sexual possessiveness or
'marital rights' as a matter for individual taste rather than communal law-making.

Some of us are liberals, and live in a (fairly) liberal society. We
tend to talk as if everybody were like us, or could be like us if only
they relaxed a bit. The implication is that, for purposes of law-
making, we can rely on the touchstone of the middle-class British

or American liberal – who, of course, doesn't mind homosexuality, dislikes capital punishment, and hates the colour bar, though he draws the line at other things. There are two snags with this. First, most people aren't liberals and do not wish to be. Homosexuality may arouse as intense feelings in them as being stolen from or assaulted. This may be mad but they don't think so. Consequently law-making is necessarily going to be, or should be, far more a matter of local conditions than the liberal theory suggests. It will have to depend on a proper sociological assessment of the forces in men's minds – on how much they can stand and how they can be educated – rather than on a vague plea 'not to interfere'. And secondly, the liberal often conceals the fact that he, too, like all of us, does draw the line at some things, and these lines may mark out oppression as well as others. A supposedly 'liberal' or 'progressive' father may turn out to be more oppressive than a Victorian one.

Questions
1. What dangers is the liberal theory of law-making supposed to avoid?
2. Should we have a law against nudity?
3. How far is sociology relevant to law-making?
4. Could you have a society without people usually telling the truth?
5. Distinguish between the meanings of 'interference' and 'influence'.
6. Do adult homosexuals 'interfere' with other people?
7. How does one distinguish a sensible view from a prejudice?

six

Justice and Fairness

---

(1) *Dear Daily . . . . . ,*
It is all very well for you to be against capital punishment, but you would feel different if it was your boy who had been killed. I say he murdered my boy, so it's only fair he should hang for it, if justice means anything.

Yours faithfully,
Unhappy Mother.

(2) *Dear Daily . . . . . ,*
It is all very well for you to be against capital punishment, but why do you suggest life imprisonment instead? I know my Johnny killed a man, but he couldn't help it, he's always had fits of temper ever since he was a child. It's not fair to punish him for what he did.

Yours faithfully,
Unhappy Mother.

(3) *Now that everyone has an equal opportunity to go to a university, no family can complain of unfair discrimination. We have abolished the criterion of wealth, and replaced it by the criterion of natural talent. As equality of opportunity increases, so too will justice and fair play.*

– Labour Party pamphlet.

(4) *You broke my bicycle so I'm going to break yours, it's only fair.*

– small child.

(5) *Sir, it's not fair, you only kept Bloggs in for half an hour, and you're keeping me in the whole afternoon, but I didn't do any more wrong than he did.*

— schoolboy.

(6) *She's so pretty she can get any boy she wants, it's not fair.*

— schoolgirl.

We're all familiar with remarks like these, and with words like 'fair', 'fair play' and 'justice'. In reading the remarks, some of us probably agree with some of them and others with others. If we're going to be honest, we shall very likely admit that which ones we agree with depends on our own preconceived ideas or prejudices. If we favour capital punishment and strict justice, we might agree with (1); if we incline to be sentimental or kind-hearted, we might agree with (2); if we vote Labour and believe in left-wing ideals, we might agree with (3), and so on. Nor do these preconceived ideas or prejudices have to take the form of moral or political beliefs, like belief in capital punishment or the abolition of capital punishment. They may be purely personal. Thus we could guess that the schoolgirl responsible for remark (6) is *not* very pretty.

Now it would be possible to translate these remarks into terms of purely personal prejudice. The 'unhappy mother' in (1) could simply say, 'I want the man who killed my boy to hang,' and the other mother in (2), 'I don't want my Johnny to suffer', and the ugly schoolgirl, 'I just hate Jane being more attractive than I am.' But, in fact, all the speakers try to justify their remarks by referring to some kind of *principle*, the principle of 'fair play' or 'justice'. The question we have to answer is exactly *what* principle this is; and it's significant that there is so much disagreement about what's fair and what's unfair. For this disagreement may stem, not from a quarrel about the facts of each particular case, but rather from a quarrel about what *counts* as fair or unfair — what the principle of fair play *is*.

Indeed these six remarks seem to imply several different principles, not just one. The first one suggests a principle of straightforward retribution, on the basis of an eye for an eye and a tooth for a tooth: if A kills B, A ought to be killed. But then the 'unhappy mother' in (2) tries to argue that her son couldn't help killing, and it wasn't his fault, which suggests that the principle has to be modified in certain cases. The Labour pamphlet in (3) implies quite a different principle, which has to do with 'equality of opportunity'. The child in (4) goes back to retribution again; and it is striking that even those of us who believe in retribution for crimes like murder – that he who kills should be killed – may well not believe that a child who breaks another's bicycle should have his own bicycle broken. The schoolboy complaining of unfairness in (5) is talking about retribution also, but not merely about that; he is complaining of *unfair* or *unequal* retribution, which seems to complicate the issue. Finally the girl in (6) implies that the pretty girl has an unfair advantage, something which enables her to be a cut above her equals.

Suppose we start with the Labour pamphlet. What has actually happened, as we know, is that the rules of our society now allow different people to go to the university from the people that used to go before 1945. At that time most people had to be rich enough, or have rich enough parents, to pay the very high fees. Now the State will pay for you if you get a place, and getting a place depends on a number of things, of which the ability to pass certain examinations, hard work, intelligence and so on are perhaps the most important. Let's simplify the position a little by saying that one criterion, wealth, has been replaced by another, intelligence.

This is thought to provide 'more equality of opportunity' and hence more fair play. But is it true that there is more equality? We might feel tempted to say that before 1945 only rich people had the chance of going to a university, and now everyone has the chance. But in fact it's not true that everyone now has the chance: people who are too stupid to pass the necessary examinations don't have a chance, any more than I have a chance of flying to the moon. There is, certainly, nothing in the laws of England which specifically states that I'm not allowed to fly to the moon, but I don't have the chance or the opportunity, simply because I can't do it; I don't have the power. In the same way, just as poor people before 1945 weren't able to go to the university because they were poor, so now stupid people can't go because they are stupid. Of course it may be a good thing, for all sorts of reasons, to use the criterion of intelligence rather than the criterion of wealth; it seems more sensible to have clever people at the university rather than rich ones. But it's not clear that this is any *fairer*.

All that has happened is that we've changed the rules of the game. It's as if we were playing a game like cricket, under certain rules. Then somebody who lacks the particular skills and talents which are useful in cricket – perhaps he's short-sighted or can't run very fast – complains that he doesn't have a fair chance to shine at this game. So we change the rules, or perhaps change the game altogether and play an indoor game instead, like cards. But now somebody who is bad at cards, perhaps because he has a bad memory or is no good at adding up, complains in just the same way. So then we change the game again; but whatever game we play, those who do not have whatever skills are needed to win will complain. Hence it seems that no game can be fairer than any other. The only way you could get a completely fair game would be to have a game which was not a game of skill at all, but a game of pure chance, like Bingo. Here all the players really do have an equal chance or an equal opportunity, because they do not use any skills or talents at all; they are either lucky or unlucky. In the same way we might think that the only really fair way to select people for the university was to draw lots.

If this is what the principle of fairness leads us to, it seems rather unfortunate, for not many of us believe that the whole of our social and political system should be conducted like a game of pure chance. But the comparison with games suggests that there is one principle that does not lead to this conclusion. If somebody cheats in a game, that is certainly unfair, because he has broken the rules. This is different from saying that the game as a whole is unfair; it is saying that the player has made an unfair move *within* the game – a move not allowed by the rules.

All references to fairness imply the existence of a set of rules within which certain things are allowed or disallowed : that is, fair or unfair. To act fairly is to act *legitimately*; to act unfairly is, essentially, to *cheat*. Differences of opinion about what is fair or unfair are really differences of opinion about what the rules are or ought to be. Sometimes we should all agree with a particular set of rules, and then we should all agree on what was fair and unfair. For instance, most of us would agree with the set of rules implied by the schoolboy in (5). The rule he is using states that, if two boys commit similar crimes, then they ought not to have different punishments, or at least that one ought not to be punished twice as much as the other. If we accept this rule, it follows that the master acted unfairly in keeping Bloggs in for half an hour, and the other boy for a whole afternoon.

The difficulty we found in trying to decide which games were fairer than others was the difficulty of deciding what set of rules should govern our choice of games. If we were all to agree that only those games should be played which favour, say, intelligence rather than brute strength, then we should agree that games like chess and bridge were fair and other games unfair. Since in fact we don't all agree about this, we seem to be reduced to games of chance which do not favour anybody.

Hence, when the Labour pamphleteer claims that one criterion (intelligence) is fairer than another (wealth), he presumably has in mind a *higher* set of rules by which to use intelligence is fair and to use wealth is cheating. Now, is there any principle which would lead us to prefer this set of rules to any other? Or is it merely that some people arbitrarily prefer one and other people another? This is what disputes concerning fairness are really about; and we can see how easy it is to turn them into mere expressions of prejudice. Obviously if you are rich it would be nice if there were a principle in virtue of which games that favoured wealth were fairer than others, and if you are intelligent you are likely to invent (if you do not already believe in) a principle whereby intelligence is a fairer criterion for university entrance than wealth. But are there such principles?

One principle might be that the rules we set up ought to depend on what we might call *natural* rather than *accidental* characteristics: that is, characteristics which are part of a person rather than those which he has acquired by chance or as a result of pre-existing social rules. For instance, qualities like intelligence, strength, determination and so on are natural characteristics; they go to make up what the person *is*. But things like being born into a rich family, or having a name with a hyphen in it, or being a hereditary aristocrat, are not really qualities at all; they are social attributes which do not form part of the person himself. If this is our principle of fairness, then it would justify selection by intelligence rather than by wealth.

But as the schoolgirl's remark in (6) shows, we sometimes object to natural characteristics as unfair, in this case, the characteristic of being very pretty. There are plenty of similar examples. We might call it unfair that some people should be born cripples, or spastics, or midgets. So we may have to make a distinction between those natural characteristics which the rules should allow to operate freely and those which they shouldn't. Remark (2) gives us some guidance here : the mother suggests that her boy *couldn't help* killing, and says that because of this it's not fair to punish him. He has a natural characteristic (bad temper) which, in her view, he can't do anything about; it is not his fault. This leads us to the principle that the rules should only take into account those natural characteristics which are within our control.

Do we actually believe in such a principle? There is some evidence that we do. Suppose we have a number of children of different ages and sizes who are all going in for a race, and we're asked to arrange the handicaps, in such a way that the race will be fair. It would certainly not be fair that the richer children, or the children who were born in Mayfair, should be given a good start; this reflects our first principle, that whatever rules we make should be based on the children's qualities and not their accidental attributes. So suppose we start them all off on the same line. We could still object that this was unfair, since some children have longer legs, greater stamina, more speed off the mark, etc., than others. If we take all these characteristics into account and adjust the handicaps accordingly, we have a situation in which – provided our handicaps are perfectly worked out – all the children would cross the finishing line at the same time *if they all try as hard as each other*.

This second principle, then, says that the fairest games are those in which only things like moral effort, trying hard, exercising one's will-power and so on are allowed to count. Thus it might be fairer (though for other reasons undesirable) to award university places not to the most intelligent but to the most conscientious or hard-working, for, as we might say, nobody can help it if he is stupid but anyone can work hard if he tries. Similarly the schoolgirl might say that the rules governing how many boy-friends a girl gets should not be framed in terms of prettiness, but perhaps in terms of how hard a girl tries to be nice to boys; not everybody can be pretty, but everybody can try to be nice.

This is not to say that we should simply disregard altogether the natural characteristics that we can't help having or not having, but we should compensate or handicap for them. Thus in the distribution of wealth we shouldn't give the most money to those who produce most goods or reach the most important positions, for this may well be due simply to their natural talents which they were born with; we should rather give it to those who work hardest. We should *expect* more from people who were naturally quick or clever and thereby, in a sense, handicap them by setting them a higher standard.

This also accounts for the fact that we often feel we ought to compensate certain people whom, as we say, life has treated unfairly. If somebody is born crippled, or spastic, or a moron, most people would think that he deserves special treatment or consideration, to make up for the 'raw deal' that life or destiny has given him. It isn't fair that people should suffer from such disadvantages, since they have done nothing to merit them; it's not their fault.

Briefly, then, we seem to think that good and bad things in life ought to be distributed to people in accordance with their *moral merits*. If nature fails to do this, which it usually does, then we must arrange matters better ourselves. This will enable us to deal with some of the remarks with which we began. The unhappy mother in (2) is justified in saying that her son should not be punished if – only if – the action he did wasn't his fault, for if it wasn't, then it can't be counted to his moral discredit, so that he ought not to receive something bad (punishment) for it. Again, the pretty girl in (6) is not morally meritorious, so that she ought not to receive the benefit of getting all the boys she wants. And the criterion of intelligence as opposed to wealth for university entrance (3) is not much fairer, since intelligence is not a moral merit, though we might say it is a bit fairer, since (unlike wealth) it is at least a natural quality rather than just a piece of good luck.

Here however we must note the position we put ourselves in, if we assent to these principles. It is perfectly reasonable to approve a social system in which intelligent (rather than hard working) people get into the university, or pretty (rather than nice) girls get more boy-friends. But we can't approve of it because it is fair, if we define what is fair in terms of moral effort only. We shall have to say things like 'Well, I admit it isn't strictly fair, but it is desirable because . . .' and then give our reasons. This is not disturbing; we do in fact often say such things in some form or another, such as, 'Really you deserve to be punished, but we'll let you off because . . .', or 'Justice demands that he suffer, but let's temper justice with mercy, because . . .' The alternative is to go back on the principle of restricting what is fair to moral merit, and relate it to other rules which we choose to suit ourselves. Thus *if we assent* to a system in which pretty girls are rewarded just because they are pretty, we can *then* say that it is fair for them to be rewarded; just as if we assent to a game of skill like bridge, then it is quite fair that the best and most talented players should win.

It doesn't much matter which alternative we take, as long as we make it clear what rules we are relating 'fair' to. In practice people often use it in reference to the existing rules of society; and these rules do very often reward other things besides moral merit – intelligence, good fortune, good looks, and so on. The more we inspect the rules, however, the more we feel inclined to restrict 'fair' to those rules which reward moral merits only, and to justify those rules which reward other things on other grounds, such as social efficiency. Hence it seems preferable to take the first alternative, and to stick to the principle we have outlined.

But we still want to know *how* to operate our principle of distribution according to moral merit. In (5), both boys are punished because they have done something wrong, but it's still unfair because they weren't punished equally even though they both did the same thing. This suggests another principle, that similar cases should be treated similarly. What counts as a similar case, however, is a very open question. For instance, if one of the boys was the ringleader and egged the other one on, it might be quite fair to punish the first more severely, even though what they actually did was exactly the same. But if we're going to distribute punishments or rewards unequally, the principle suggests that we have to show a good reason for it; to put it loosely, we can't just dish out any old punishment or reward we like.

One kind of good reason that is universally accepted is that the worse the behaviour, the worse the punishment should be; the better the behaviour, the better the reward. (The same is true of moral intentions and motives, as well as behaviour; that's why attempted murder is a crime as well as murder – we are still concerned with the moral merits of the case, not just the act itself.) We thus have a kind of scale by which we measure crimes and punishments, and make them balance as much as we can : murder is punished more than theft, and theft more than parking a car in the wrong place.

The simplest version of such a scale is found in (1) and (4). This is the 'eye for an eye, tooth for a tooth' version, where the punishment exactly 'fits' (is equal to) the crime. I kill somebody, somebody else kills me; I break your bicycle, you break mine. Such a scale is perfectly fair or just, but it is not the *only* scale that can be fair and just, and one might object to it on other grounds (e.g. that it doesn't do much to reform the criminal, that it's barbaric, and so on). We might prefer a system whereby a criminal is made to do hard labour, or go through a course of remedial treatment. But if what we do to him is fair, it must be something at least slightly unpleasant; otherwise it is not in accordance with his moral merits. If I commit a crime and am rewarded with a long holiday with pay as a result, this cannot be fair or just, not because it would be bad for me or bad for society, but simply because it does not follow the principle of distribution according to merit.

Here again, if we do not believe in retributive punishment and reward it is best to say straight out that this principle is perfectly fair, but not desirable on other grounds. In that case we should probably not believe in punishments and rewards at all, though we might believe in deterrents and incentives, like sticks and carrots for a donkey. We can only punish and reward somebody *for* something, i.e. in requital or retribution for something; the words 'punish' and 'reward' make no sense except in a context of fairness and justice. It is one thing to *treat* criminals *in the light of* their crimes, and another to *punish* them *for* their crimes: the first suggests that criminals should be dealt with as if they were ill or diseased, and the second that they should be dealt with as moral agents, according to the principles of justice.

Finally, *why* should we accept this principle of fairness? Most people regard it as so obviously desirable that it passes without question, and certainly it is very deeply rooted in human nature – even very young children accept it, like the child in (4). But that in itself is not a very good reason; there may be all sorts of things that are deeply rooted in human nature, but nevertheless undesirable. Thus some people have suggested that to believe in retributive punishment is just a piece of vindictiveness or the desire for revenge. But this seems too simple, for it is as much a question of rewarding the good as of punishing the bad – and this suggests a deeply-rooted *moral* principle, not just a selfish desire.

In practice, as well as in theory, we can't believe that we ought to reward the good but not punish the bad, or that it's fair to do this. We can't believe it in theory, because 'fair' implies the distribution of all things, good and bad, according to merit; and we can't do it in practice, because to reward the good is in effect to punish the bad. Suppose, for instance, that we have just enough food to go round, as is actually the case in many societies. Then if we use up some of it as a reward for those who behave well or work hardest, some of those who have not behaved or worked properly will, in effect, be punished by having to go short. You cannot create a privileged or 'rewarded' group without at the same time creating an underprivileged or 'punished' group.

One obvious reason for the principle of fairness is that punishments and rewards do usually act as deterrents and incentives. We might think that, if we didn't punish the wicked there would be more crimes committed, and if we didn't reward the hard-working, people would do less work. Another equally obvious reason is that punishments and rewards act beneficially on the individuals punished and rewarded : the criminal is taught that crime does not pay, and the virtuous person that virtue does pay. But it can be shown that these are not the only reasons. In practice, we know very little about how much our punishments and rewards do actually operate as good encouragements, deterrents, incentives and so on. There may well be cases where they are not effective in this way at all. Yet we might still believe that *some* punishment or reward was desirable.

The basic reason is hard to state exactly, but seems to have something to do with the notion of *compensation*. If a player in a game cheats by taking two turns running, we are likely to make him miss his turn next time round. Our motives for doing this are not solely to make him think twice before cheating again, or to deter other people from cheating as he has cheated. It's more a matter of *levelling up* the situation. In committing a crime, the criminal gets away with something, and we compensate for this by taking something away from him (like the cheat in the game). In the same way, a virtuous person gives society something which perhaps costs him an effort; we compensate him by a reward. It's as if we regarded all human beings as equals, under a set of rules. If you don't compensate for a breach of the rules, the game can't continue; anyone can do as he likes, and it is no longer a game but a free-for-all. We could put this by saying that everyone has an equal right to the good things of life, and if he gets more or less than his share, we ought to equalise the position by subtraction or addition. Retribution of moral merits is only one instance of this general principle; as we saw earlier, we think it right to compensate for the disadvantages of those born crippled or spastic, irrespective of their moral merits.

It may well be asked why we should accept this fundamental human equality. A short answer can be given by saying that, if we are to think morally and rationally at all, rather than after the manner of Hitler or some other fanatic, we have to begin by accepting other human beings as equals. If I'm prepared to count everybody but myself as something less than human – as if they were born slaves, or natural inferiors, or just animals – then I have no need of a morality, nor of any principles of fairness; I simply do what I want with them. Morality starts with the acceptance of equality; the need for moral principles arises from a situation in which there are equals, but a conflict of interests. We might still ask, 'Why think morally?' or 'Why be rational?' But this is another question.

Questions
1. Consider the following words: rich, aristocratic, intelligent, bad-tempered, lazy, stupid, cowardly, red-haired, English, determined, neurotic, middle-class, literate, ugly, sulky.
   (*a*) Which of them describe (i) social attributes; (ii) natural characteristics; (iii) moral characteristics?
   (*b*) Which ones do you have serious doubts about, when you consider how they ought to be categorized? Why do the doubts arise?
2. 'Every Englishman has an equal chance of being Prime Minister.' Is this true?

3. Is retributive punishment merely vindictive?
4. If I positively enjoy being good, should I be rewarded?
5. Is it fair to punish kleptomaniacs for stealing?
6. (*a*) 'It's just, but it's not right'; (*b*) 'It's just, but it's not fair.' Say for each case whether the remark is intelligible, and if so what it means.
7. If there is a God, does he give everybody a fair deal?

III
CONCEPTS AND THE
HUMAN INDIVIDUAL

seven

Mental Health and the Unconscious Mind

In this chapter I want to discuss only one aspect of 'mental health', and in order to do this clearly we must first identify another aspect, if only to lay it aside. This second aspect concerns 'mental disease' in a sense exactly parallel with 'physical disease', that is, something which is produced by physical causes and can be cured by physical methods. For instance, if a man has a tumour of the brain, or is given certain drugs, or gets a severe injury on the head, he may become 'mentally ill' as a result, and he may be cured, perhaps, by an operation on his brain or by other drugs.

There is no particular philosophical interest in this sort of case. More interesting, and also more difficult, are those cases of 'mental health' which relate to the kind of talk which psycho-analysts and others have produced since Freud. Psycho-analysts say startling things like, 'He thinks he loves his mother, but really he hates her as well', or, 'The reason why he always has rows with his boss is that unconsciously he is still trying to escape from his father's domination'. These unconscious reasons, according to the psycho-analysts, are operative in all of us. But not all of us, of course, are mentally ill. It is only when these unconscious reasons so affect our thinking and behaviour that it becomes highly undesirable and abnormal that we talk of 'mental illness'.

By 'undesirable' and 'abnormal', of course, we must not simply mean 'what our society thinks undesirable' or 'unlike what most people think and do', i.e. not normal in the sense of not average. For what society thinks undesirable, or what is not average, may nevertheless be perfectly right and proper. Thus in a Nazi or Fascist society 'normal' (i.e. average) behaviour would consist in tolerating the slaughter of millions of Jews; but this would not be *right* behaviour. We must mean something more like *unreasonable*, or irrational, behaviour. It would have to be unreasonable to a very high degree, of course, to count as mental *illness*. A lunatic who thinks he is Napoleon, or a man who feels compelled to touch every lamp-post in the street, or a person who can't stop himself from taking drugs, would be unreasonable to this degree.

Now the interesting thing about these cases of mental illness is that psychiatrists give these odd-sounding reasons for them, reasons in terms of the 'unconscious' mind. One way of trying to make sense of these reasons is to try and consider whether psycho-analysts can sensibly claim to know more about our own reasons than we do ourselves. Since Freud, a great many people who would otherwise have been secure in the belief that they felt this, or wanted that, are impressed by the beliefs of psycho-analytic theorists that what they *really* feel (want, fear) is different from what they think they feel. Most people, in fact, are doubtful about these claims. Sometimes they think, 'Well, I think I love her, but if the psycho-analyst says I hate her, I suppose it must be true.' But sometimes they think, 'Damn it, *I'm* the one who knows what I feel, whatever the psycho-analyst says.'

There is one obvious way in which claims to know other people better than they know themselves can be true. Biologists know more about my body than I do, for example. So we feel tempted to say that psychologists know more about my mind. And there's a sense in which this is obviously true too; indeed, you don't have to be a psychologist to know more about somebody else than he does. A good schoolmaster has a better idea of a boy's mental capabilities than the boy does. He can predict, better than the boy, how he will perform in an examination. If he's very observant, he can also predict what sort of friends the boy will make, what sort of job he will do, whether he will be a good boy or get into trouble, and so on. Yet we still feel that there is *something* which only we know best about ourselves.

Suppose a man in love with a girl says, 'She makes me so happy', and is not lying. But we see him going around with a long face, trembling with fear whenever he meets her, and generally betraying all the signs of misery. We say to him, 'You're not really happy, you only think you are.' He says, 'Well, if I think I'm happy then I *am* happy.' How do we settle this? What *we* mean is that he is misdescribing his feelings, that the appropriate word for what he feels, if he will own up to it, is not 'happy', but perhaps 'tense', 'excited', 'romantically obsessed' or whatever. And here *we* are right. What *he* means, perhaps, is partly that, whatever the appropriate description of his feelings may be, he has decided to go along with them; that he is in favour of his state of mind and doesn't intend to change it for another. And in this *he* is right.

We might represent this by saying, 'A man can be wrong about his feelings, but at least he can't be wrong about his own intentions or choices.' But this may mean various things. Jesus said, 'Father, forgive them, for they know not what they do.' Now this might mean:

(1) That they were just acting blindly, for no reason, not really *acting* at all, but just blundering along, as an elephant might not know that it was trampling down a cornfield (because elephants don't *know* things at all). But this is obviously wrong. The people who put Jesus on the cross knew quite well, in one way, what they were doing. They had certain intentions and purposes, which they might have phrased as 'getting rid of a blasphemer', 'punishing a criminal' or 'maintaining the orthodox religion'.

(2) It might mean that they were ignorant of some fact: that what they were actually doing was killing the Son of God, but they didn't know he was the Son of God, so they didn't know what they were doing. But this is not to claim that they were ignorant of their own intentions, only that they were ignorant of some vital fact that might have made them change their minds (just as a nice elephant wouldn't trample down a cornfield if it knew it was a cornfield).

(3) It might mean that *their* description of their intentions was incorrect, and that a better description was, perhaps, 'getting rid of somebody who threatened them', or 'taking revenge'. But how can we say this? If what they had in mind was the description 'getting rid of a blasphemer', then isn't that their intention, rather than 'getting rid of a threat' or 'taking revenge'? And of course in a sense it is. This is the sense in which people are the only real authorities about what they intend. They knew better than anyone else what they said to themselves; they said, 'let's get rid of that blasphemer'.

But in another sense perhaps they didn't know what they had in mind. And this is not to say that they were subject to certain pulls or pushes in their minds, called perhaps 'the urge to remove threats' or 'a drive for revenge' (like a feeling of faintness, or depression, or high spirits); it is to say that they did have in mind, without being fully aware of it, certain *descriptions*, conceptually formulated, like 'getting rid of a threat'. They identified Jesus as a threat, and *therefore* decided to get rid of him. The 'therefore' represents the fact that they were following a rule, rather than just blundering along, or just being driven by unformulated urges. In other words, *people can follow rules unconsciously.* And in this sense, they may not know as well as another person what they intend. Much the same arguments apply to the notion of unconscious wants, desires and choices.

We could not talk in this way if we did not believe (as some do not) that a man can consciously formulate a rule (intention, desire, etc.), forget or repress it, and yet still follow it. Yet one does not have to be a convinced Freudian to see that this is so. It is quite understandable that one should formulate a desire to take revenge, object consciously to such desires for revenge as a matter of principle, and hence pretend to oneself that one does not have it, understandable that one should nevertheless continue to follow it, and hence understandable that one should try to redescribe it in more fair-seeming terms, such as 'a desire for justice' or 'righteous indignation'.

It is for these reasons that it is misleading to regard psycho-analysis solely in such terms as 'cure', 'disease', 'therapy', etc. For a man's intention, even if unconscious, are part of him in a much stronger sense than his diseases are. Characteristically, psycho-analysts do not say, 'Poor chap, you have a complex/trauma/fixation. I'll see if I can get rid of it for you', as doctors might get rid of warts. Their general line is, 'You are seeing things wrong; you have lost touch with your own intentions; you misdescribe your own feelings; you fail to remember your past decisions; you do not know what you are doing.' People may be forgiven for this kind of blindness, just because they do not know what they are doing, but it is still *they* who are doing it.

This is why certain methods of trying to prove a psycho-analytic theory are often likely to miss the point. If I say, 'He smokes because he was weaned early', I may be offering a general law of cause and effect, which can be verified by normal scientific methods. But if I say, 'They killed him because (unconsciously) they wanted to get rid of a threat', this is offering something more like a *historical* explanation, an explanation in terms of formu-lated purposes, desires and intentions. 'Why did Brutus kill Caesar?', as asked by a historian, is a demand for Brutus's reasons and intentions, not a demand for some general law (say) to the effect that republicans always kill tyrants, a law quite independent of whatever may go on in the heads of republicans.

One of the best ways to establish a purposive explanation is to get the person to admit it himself; and this is what has tempted some psycho-analysists to say that you can only see the truth of their contentions by being psycho-analysed yourself, i.e. by taking part in a form of communication in which your admissions will be more honest than usual. But it is not the only way; even though only Brutus may be the ultimate authority about his intentions, we can make very good guesses about them. The fact that he is dead does not destroy the whole possibility of historical explana-tion, any more than the fact that we cannot remember our own past histories destroys psycho-analytic explanation.

Nor would we say that we can always feel *more certain* about scientific or causal explanation than about purposive explanation or anything else to the effect that the second type of explanation is somehow inferior ('not really scientific', 'not properly proved'). Such explanations can be properly proved, only not by the same method of proof. They are not inferior; they are just different. Granted that many psycho-analysts, including Freud, propounded many of their explanations as if they were causal; granted that *some* of their explanations should be regarded as causal (and it is a very different problem to know which these are – perhaps those which refer to the prelinguistic stage of childhood?); and granted that it is still very fashionable to be as 'empirical' or 'scientific' as possible; we still have really no excuse for dismissing psycho-analytic explanation on the grounds that it is not 'scientific', or 'not experimentally verifiable'. I know that the explanation for my wife going out is that she wants to buy a new hat. I don't need an experiment to verify this; no experiment could. I know because she tells me, and because I know that she is in no sense speaking dishonestly.

The sense in which psycho-analysts may know more about us than we know about ourselves is in one way more worrying than the sense in which (say) biologists do, but in another way it is less worrying. If I am told that a disease is 'psychosomatic' (meaning here that it is in some sense the result of my own intentions, of a false or escapist world-view) I might think (1) 'Oh, Lord, that means I can't get it put right quickly by an injection or a couple of tablets'. But I might think (2) 'Oh, good, that means that if I try to see things differently, or face facts, or be honest, I can re-educate (and hence cure) myself'. If the disease was, say, cancer, for which we haven't in fact got any injections or tablets, then we might well be encouraged along the lines of (2) rather than discouraged along the lines of (1).

More generally, there is a sense in which it is nice to be able to disclaim responsibility, because it costs less effort. You can say, 'Oh, well, that's how I am', or, 'You can't change human nature', and as long as you aren't being actively and overtly immoral, you can get away with it. But in fact *human* nature (which is mostly

learned, and closely connected with the concepts of language and
intention) is one of the things we can always try to change. Just
because changing our human identity is a matter of re-education
rather than being operated on, of increased rationality rather than
(in a simple sense) increased health, there is a part of the work
which only we can (logically) do for ourselves. To be taught,
rather than cured, requires a free and active learner. Psycho-
analysis stands, both in practice and theory, very much on the
borderline between morals and medicine.

Questions
1. How many different things could be meant by 'abnormal' or
   'unnatural'?
2. 'They aren't really happily married, they only think they are.' Is
   this sense?
3. Do historians explain things in the same way that scientists do?
4. What is the difference between causes and purposes?
5. Could catching a cold be 'psychosomatic'?
6. In what sense do elephants (or other animals) *know* things?
7. Does the word 'Why . . . ?' have different senses?

eight

Men and Machines

I WANT HERE to talk about a problem that arises from a consideration of robots and self-regulating machines. This problem may be roughly formulated in the question, 'What can men do that machines can't?'

Now we can take this question as roughly equivalent to questions like 'Are men machines?', 'Could we build a man?', or 'What are the differences between men and robots?' Answering these questions might calm the anxiety of someone whose doubts take the form of, 'My goodness, am I just a machine?' or, 'Good heavens, as far as I can see human beings are just robots'. These are doubts about human freedom, or about the humanity of man in general. We attempt to calm them, either by showing that there are special features that human beings have and robots don't have, or else by showing that, although human beings are indeed just very complicated machines, this isn't at all worrying.

Whichever line we take, however (and it is not at all clear that the two lines really *are* different), it is possible or even probable that we shall admit to the possibility of constructing robots which can do everything that human beings can do. And from this it is a short step to admitting that we might build various robots that can do any specific job that we care to name *better* than human beings can; not that any robot will be able to do any and every job better, but that there is no job which *some* robot will not be able to do better. This, though I want to say more about it later, should be sufficient to show the nature of the worry I am talking about. It is a worry that human beings may become *unnecessary*. We are afraid that what is happening to factory workers as a result of automation may happen to all of us as a result of similar advances in science. It is not the (surely rather silly) fear that men are just robots; it is the perfectly real fear that future robots will make future men unnecessary. For what will they be able to do that the robots can't do better? Worse, what will they be able to *be* that robots can't *be* better?

It is often hard to say just what is at stake in disputes about men and machines. Sometimes such disputes seem purely verbal. 'A' says, 'Robots can only do what you programme them to do'; 'B' replies, 'So can human beings, education and environment are just forms of programming'; and 'A' says, 'Oh, well, if that's all you mean by programming, then I can accept what you say without feeling worried.' Or 'B' says, 'You can build machines to do everything that men can do'; 'A' replies, 'Well, you might be able to build entities to do this, but then I shouldn't call them machines', and 'B' says, 'Oh, well, if that's what we're going to mean by "machine", I withdraw.'

Characteristic of such disputes, even when they are not seen to hinge merely on the use of words like 'machine', 'build', 'programme' and so on, is that people take sides. 'A' says, 'Men aren't machines, because machines can't think/feel/have intentions/be self-conscious.' 'B' replies, 'Well, presumably human beings work on *some* system; and whatever the system is, we could in principle build it.' 'A' says, 'Yes, but in a sense we can do that already, by the normal processes of human reproduction.' 'B' replies, 'Exactly, and we could do it in other ways; there's no magic in the process.' 'A' says, 'Oh, well, of course human beings don't work by magic, nobody ever said they did, so we're arguing about nothing.'

But something has been achieved even by this. For it certainly has been believed, that human beings do work by magic. It is as if we thought in three categories: cause and effect, pure chance or randomness, and magic. We can't find a place for human freedom and dignity in the first two categories, so we use the third. Either human beings are just cogs and levers, we feel, and there's no freedom there, or else they just act randomly, and there's a sort of freedom there, but not the sort we want because there's no responsibility attached to it, and so we fall back on magic. Perhaps there is a sort of little inner man at work behind the cogs and levers (the will? the consciousness? the ability to try or intend or decide?). But then as soon as we see this clearly, we see also that this merely starts the whole problem off again, for how does the little man work? So we abandon magic – even though it continues to exercise a strong unconscious influence over us.

But then we hardly know what to say. For both sides seem to be asserting the same thing. Both 'A' and 'B' want to assert that actions and thoughts flow from what people are; only 'A' wants to add 'and not just from their past history, but from themselves', thereby asserting the reality of freedom, praise, blame, responsibility, etc., and 'B' wants to add 'and not from anything magical', thereby asserting the possibility of a scientific approach to human beings. 'A' is anxious to stop 'B' from saying that men are *just* machines, for then 'B' would be missing important points; in the same way that someone who said that the psalms were *just* poetry, or poetry was *just* a collection of words, would be missing important points. 'B' is anxious to stop 'A' from saying that men are machines-plus, because this would be to introduce magic.

This comes out quite well in the notion of programming machines to do things. We want a new airliner. We feed a machine with data : a pause, and the airliner is invented. Has the machine 'only done what we programmed it to do'? Obviously there is a sense in which it has and another sense in which it hasn't. We programmed it to design *a* plane, but we didn't programme it to design *the* actual plane which it ended up by producing. The machine did that itself, that's why we built it. If it's a good machine it produces a good plane, better perhaps than anything we could invent; in a sense it has a mind of its own, and because of the complexity of the factors involved we might not be able to predict what sort of plane it would turn out. 'A' has to admit that there's nothing in the machine – no little man – which hasn't at some time been put in it by construction and programming, and 'B' has to admit that there's an important sense in which the machine isn't *just* the sum of its parts, but has a mind of its own and makes its own choices.

But now, we have been talking as if we had already decided that human beings were only machines. Suppose we use another kind of talk, and speak not of *brains* but *minds*. 'Mind', like plenty of other words, isn't intended to function within the scientific vocabulary at all. We have a language which is not intended to describe human beings as natural phenomena. 'The infinite variety of the human mind' sounds plausible, where 'The infinite variety of the human brain doesn't; we *know* brains aren't infinite. We know that human beings *can* be approached natural-istically or scientifically, and no intelligent person could deny this without committing himself to magic. But we also know that there is a kind of talk we use, about or *to* human beings, which is different from scientific talk. It is *non*-scientific, not *anti*-scientific. (You can call a ship 'she' and still do your navigation properly.)

It is important not to be frightened into thinking that scientific talk is the *only* justifiable kind of talk, into thinking that men are *just* machines and not men at all. And perhaps people have really thought this, just as they have believed in magic. But we must be careful, because of the temptation to go back on what we have established, to try and sneak in some actual power or faculty which human beings (as an observable fact) possess, while simul-taneously claiming that this faculty is immune from the cause-and-effect process, and can't really be observed or explained at all. We can't have it both ways.

The scientist says, 'You name it, I'll build it.' And now we can certainly say, 'There are some words, in talk of a certain kind about human beings, that don't name things; and if there aren't things, you can't build them.' But this is cold comfort, for there are lots of other words which do name things, or at least which clumsily describe parts or aspects of the human mechanism. Just as 'conscience' can be replaced by 'superego', and perhaps ulti-mately by a strictly scientific description, so too with words and phrases like 'rationality', 'human purposes', and 'self-control'. Of course some of these words may function in other kinds of talk as well: we shall, no doubt, always be able to *say*, 'It goes against my conscience' and not *simply* mean something that would be more accurately expressed in scientific language. There's no reason why all such terms should be intended merely as descriptions. But this still leaves us with the feeling that, when we have separated out these kinds of talk, the machine-designers will have gained an awful lot of human territory. They will have designed machines not to prove to us that we are not (as we foolishly believed) human, but to prove that we are human *and that parts and aspects of our humanity make scientific sense*. And now we are worried, not about whether we are human, but about whether our humanity is any longer of any use to us, and if so, of what use.

We are accustomed to regard machines as tools : devices, as the Greek derivation implies, to get us what we want. This must be understood in relation to thinking of a certain kind, which we can roughly describe as thinking in terms of ends and means. It has been partly the need for survival and material improvement that has led human beings – and some races of men more than others – to conceive their lives as purposive in a very strong sense of the word. We give ourselves certain ends (money, fame, power, security), ends which we often know quite well that we shall not achieve in the near future : that is, we prefer to regard our present activities purposively, as activities in which we engage *in order* to achieve something. It is the kind of culture which lays stress on purposiveness, in this sense, which has in fact produced and developed the machine.

It is partly because of this that we become worried as soon as we recognize the problem that machines pose us. For if not merely some activities, but *any* activity, which men undertake can be undertaken by a machine instead, it will seem that we have no *raison d'être*. We assume that human activities must be purposive; indeed, perhaps we are even accustomed to regard purposiveness as a distinguishing mark of rationality and humanity. Therefore it seems that the purposes can be achieved by machines rather than by men. If we walk in order to arrive, work in order to earn money, or tackle philosophical problems in order to solve them, we shall be out of a job, for we have already invented cars, we are on the way to achieving economic security by the use of mechanical devices, and perhaps soon someone will invent a machine that solves philosophical problems.

We may admit that we are often uncertain about the application of the end-means mode of thought. I may walk merely in order to arrive, or partly in order to arrive and partly for pleasure, or purely for pleasure. I may do my work because I think it is good for me, or tackle philosophical problems because it keeps my brain active. It might be thought, therefore, that these are (at least) as much ends as means, and that no machine can ever take them away from us. But the machine-designer can say, 'If I can design a machine to give you the pleasure and benefit of walking or working without your actually *doing* those things, would that not be just as good?' And now it seems very difficult to say that it would *not* be just as good.

We are thus driven to consider, in a somewhat unusual form, the question of what forms of activity or modes of existence we regard as valuable or desirable in themselves. Let us suppose that we agree about these forms, and call them by the general title of 'happiness'. Then the position will be that we could have a happiness-producing machine, or if not precisely a machine, a combination perhaps of drugs, brain-surgery, and so on. The machine would so alter our external environment and improve our inner selves that we could spend our whole time in the desired state. We are accustomed to regard machines and drugs, and perhaps particularly brain-surgery, as remedies for which a price has to be paid : we cut a nerve in the brain, and this makes the man more contented, but only at the cost of decreasing his awareness. But this is a sign only of our present clumsiness. We can build an awareness-producing machine if we are clever enough, and so with any activity, faculty, or state of mind. Whatever we choose to call happiness, we can produce it artificially.

So far this is not very worrying. We might, indeed, have thought that what counts in life is the strife and the struggle, the fight to overcome difficulties, so that the machine, which acts as a kind of immediate wish-fulfilment device, might seem to knock the bottom out of our views of life as a kind of assault course. But, first, it seems that this view is an odd one; it is as if we said that trying to get to heaven was better than being there. And, secondly, if we really insist on having a battle, we can build this into the machine too. We might feel, then, that all was well; the machine is merely a rather more efficient extension of ordinary tools, which we use to hasten our achievement of happiness. It is true that there is no longer any place for efforts which are unassisted by mechanism; if aspirations, seeking, striving, etc., are valuable we would build them into the machine, because the machine would give them to us more efficiently than we could give them to ourselves. But the machines still serve humanity; that is, they serve human nature and human choices.

But then we notice that machines could handle human nature and human choice as well. What we now fear is a machine, not that gives us happiness, but that *tells us what it is*. Rational choice of what to do, or how to be happy, depends on a knowledge of the facts (particularly the facts of human nature), and on the ability to choose without prejudice or bias. On both these counts other people, and also a machine, can be superior to ourselves. A properly programmed machine could both know what we were like better than we did, and also make the kind of choice that we would make if we were not disturbed by the human obstacles of prejudice and bias, or other obstacles such as lack of time, patience, or the ability to concentrate.

We must add to this the possibility that human nature itself can be changed. Now we are faced, not only by a machine that produces happiness for men, but also by a machine that alters men, perhaps to fit a new picture of happiness. Thus perhaps a machine will say, 'Men will never be really happy unless they are telepathic', and we shall wake up one day to find that we know what everyone else is thinking. All these possibilities make us wonder whether we can still call these machines *tools*. They seem to have taken over our lives completely.

We may split this worry into two questions. The first is, 'Are we being dictated to?' In one sense, of course we are; in so far as we commit ourselves to machines at all, we are in some sense in their power. But this is as true when we accept the answer of a simple adding machine as when we accept the answer of the happiness machine. We trust the machine to do certain jobs for us; if it gets the answers wrong, we suffer. But there is one sense in which we cannot, unless we choose, be dictated to, for we are not bound to *commit* ourselves to machines. Even if we allow a machine to alter our personalities, tell us what happiness is for these new personalities, and forthwith put us in the state of happiness, the initial act of choice will be our own. We might even commit ourselves to machines that put us in the hands of other machines, and so on, but the original committal is still ours. Hence the anxiety about whether we can retain power over our machines in a quite straightforward sense of being able to control them, is genuine but not indissoluble. We need to be careful, because if the machines are stronger than we they can prevent us from making our commitments; but their mere existence in itself does not remove our freedom. Indeed, like the existence of all other tools, it can enlarge it.

The second question is, 'What can we do or be by our own efforts?'; and part of the answer to this is the same. In a sense, when we use a machine we are not making our own efforts; but in another sense we are. What we are doing is to make, as it were, sophisticated efforts : we are, simply, using tools to achieve our ends. Since men always use tools of some kind, even if only the tools of language and symbols, there is (if we want to press the point) a sense in which we never do anything purely by our own efforts, i.e. without the help of any tools. But this sense is not worrying.

However, this is only part of the answer, for some tools and machines cut out certain human activities altogether. If we drive instead of walk, we certainly travel and arrive by our own efforts, but we do not walk by our own efforts since we do not walk at all. From what we have seen it appears that no *specific* activity is safe.

And this is true. All that is safe is the activity or state of being our-selves. If we put our money on any means (rather than ends), or on any kind of becoming (rather than being), we shall infallibly lose it; and equally if we put our money on any specific kind of end or any specific mode of being, we shall lose it too. Machines can do everything that we do, make us into anything we let them, and even be anything that we are. *But they cannot be us.* What 'being ourselves' consists of is a completely open question, but whatever answer we give ourselves or allow machines to give us, there is one sense in which we necessarily live our own lives.

I do not, of course, intend to suggest either (*a*) that science will in fact make sufficient advances to face us with actual machines of this kind, or (*b*) that our world will ever become *completely* mechanized in the way I have described; it is, rather, a condition which we gradually approach. But the possibility of a mechaniza-tion which is virtually complete, and the certainty of increasing mechanization, are sufficient to make us revise a great deal of our thinking. Thus, if we take the concept of work to imply the notion of a means toward an end (we toil *in order to* survive and grow rich), then in the course of time we may find that we have to think of human activity in other terms: in the category of play, for instance. Do we play in order to enjoy ourselves, or do we just play? If we just play, this looks like a category that will survive mechanization. Again, do we want the process of striving and achieving – building up tension and then releasing it – or do we want a state of tensionless calm? Either can be produced in us mechanically, no doubt, but perhaps the concept of tension, like play, is part and parcel of the concept of a living organism. It is to such questions as these that this problem gives point and focus.

Questions
1. Do adding machines really add, in the same sense that human beings add? How about chess-playing machines?

2. Is education just a kind of programming?
3. Could you build a human being?
4. 'He did it for the money'; 'He did it for pleasure.' Are these two statements parallel?
5. Could a machine write poetry? Feel pain? Pray? Fall in love?
6. Are human beings unpredictable?
7. 'Machines don't have souls.' Do men? What does 'soul' mean?

nine

Language and Society

ONE SIGNIFICANT difference – perhaps ultimately the most significant – between man and the other animals is that man is psychologically and sociologically more flexible than they. This mental flexibility can be expressed in various ways. We can say that animals are tied down to a comparatively rigid system of behaviour-patterns and instincts and responses to stimuli, whereas man has free choice and intelligence; or we can say that animals are unconscious of what they are doing, whereas man is conscious and aware; or we can say that animals use only their natural resources, whereas man is capable of using tools. But one of the most illuminating ways of putting the point is to say that man alone is capable of controlling his environment and himself by means of language-techniques.

A language, in the strict sense, is an artificial and consciously-organized method of control by the use of symbols or conventions, which involves the notion of meaning. The behaviour of animals satisfies some of these criteria, but not all : thus beavers control their environment artificially, but not by the use of symbols, and rooks communicate (in some sense) to each other by making various sounds, but this is not a consciously-organized language. None of the actions or signs of animals have meaning in the sense that they are consciously agreed and understood as symbols; and this, we might say, is why the so-called languages of animals are inflexible, or not really languages at all.

Without going too deeply into the matter, we can see that there are various senses of 'meaning', as of 'communications', which do not satisfy these conditions. Thus, if a man licks his lips, it is correct to say that this 'means' he is hungry; dark clouds 'mean', or are signs of, rain; a handshake 'means' that someone wants to be friends; a husband's bad temper over the breakfast table may 'mean' lack of sexual satisfaction on the previous night; and so forth. None of these, however, are agreed and artificial symbols, consciously used, and none of them are cases of communication in this narrow sense. Thus, to take a further example, a kiss may be a communication in the sense that the people who kiss react on each other in certain ways, have certain feelings and intentions, etc., and also no doubt in the sense that they both 'share the same feeling' (though it is not clear what this means exactly). But a kiss need not be a communication in the narrow sense, for it may not be used or understood as a symbol); it may be just a kiss.

The whole point of having a language, of course, is precisely that it *is* artificial and can therefore give us more control than less flexible natural methods. This becomes most obvious if we consider, say, trying to solve a problem about measuring water by pouring it into different jugs of different capacities. Here the 'natural' method is to deal directly with actual jugs and actual water; but this is cumbersome and tedious, and the artificial method of using pencil and paper and playing around with figures is more efficient. Here we use, in a simple or advanced form, a *notation*, and the importance of notation in mathematics is well known. Again, we could consider the invention and development of maps. Like every other language, maps act as an artificial intermediary between ourselves and the real world; they are one method of reducing the real world to manageable proportions, of extracting and identifying certain features of the real world, inventing artificial signs for them and representing them in a convenient form. The more informative and useful the map, the more artificial and the less naturalistic it tends to be; dragons and cherubs puffing their cheeks tend to disappear, to be replaced by the artificialities of contour lines and conventional signs of other sorts. We can think also of the greater degree of abstraction reached by advanced as against primitive languages, and of modern physics as against Newtonian physics; in both these cases the language becomes less like a simple representation of the out-side world, in terms of objects we can picture, and more like a set of useful symbols, no one of which necessarily 'stands for' a 'thing' in the world, in the sense in which proper names 'stand for' the things or people to which they refer.

The usefulness of increased artificiality is apparent in at least two different ways. First, it allows greater discrimination and a higher degree of specification. Thus, if we remove the cheek-puffing cherubs, we leave room for symbols indicating the strength, duration and direction of winds; and by inventing arti-ficial signs like $\frac{1}{4}$ or $\frac{3}{4}$ we allow ourselves to specify more than we can specify by the use of whole numbers alone. Secondly, it allows increased possibility of generalization and classification : thus by moving from arithmetic to algebra, from 1, 2 and 3 to x, y and z, we can generalize about numbers more freely, and by inventing words like 'object' and 'symmetry' we can say things that we could not otherwise say, not at least without considerable difficulty. In-creased control over our environment, or new and creative think-ing, is not only always accompanied by a new terminology; in an important sense the discovery of a new terminology is part of the invention and the increased control. Anyone who invents some-thing or discovers something thereby makes sense, as it were, of a part of our environment which did not make sense before : he identifies its features, names them, maps them, turns them from meaninglessness into language. He brings them under conscious control, enables us to keep tabs on them.

Any improvement of control is thus an improvement in con-sciousness, and any improvement in consciousness is an improve-ment in language. The process of thinking is itself linguistic or symbolic; it is a scaled-down version of acting or doing something, in which we move small quantities of energy around on a map in order to see the probable outcome of various courses of action. Many psychologists have put this by saying that our thinking should be rational or realistic rather than 'autistic' (self-centred) or magical, and this is to say that the symbols and meaning of our thoughts should connect closely with reality, and not be merely the magical projections of our own unconscious fears and desires. If we are masters of our own symbols, using them artificially to suit our own convenience, we act freely; if we become dominated or bewitched by them, we act and think compulsively. The processes of philosophical or psychological analysis, and to a great extent of other ways of thinking also, are designed to free us from bewitchment; to make what is unconscious conscious; to give us a clearly-understood language in which to solve our problems. Thus a neurotic problem in psycho-analysis, or a problem in philosophy, is precisely a problem whose chief difficulty consists in our own unawareness of what we are saying, in a lack of self-consciousness about language. The neurotic *says* things, but plainly he does not (in one sense) *mean* them; there is a fatal gap between the language he uses consciously and the unconscious features of his personality which he is unable to identify and express in linguistic form, and his cure consists precisely in giving him a language which will enable him to incorporate those features into his conscious mind and hence to handle them in whatever way he chooses. It is a matter of getting the unconscious features to *own up*, as it were. So too in philosophical problems: by linguistic analysis we have to bring whatever is at the back of our minds to the front, so as to bring it under the conscious control of a language.

We could put this point another way by saying that we exercise control over ourselves and our environment in so far as *we* give meaning to features in the world, rather than simply allowing these features to 'mean' things to us – or as we ought rather to say, allowing them to act on us as inevitable stimuli. Animals do not handle reality at all; they merely react to it. Men can handle it, but only by the medium of language. Belief in features of the environment or of ourselves that have some kind of independent or magical power or existence – such as belief in fairies or demons, in metaphysical or moral absolutes ('Truth', 'Beauty', etc.) which are supposed to have independent existence, and many others – can thus be regarded as a failure of language. In these cases there is a sense in which *we* give meaning to these features: that is, we invest them with magical properties and powers. But this is an un-consciously-inspired process: the features act upon our uncon-scious minds, which in turn project parts of themselves upon the features. Thus we make our gods, our lovers and even some objects in the physical world in the image of our own minds. We do not *choose* meanings for them, in the same sense that we choose, for instance, that a certain stone shall be the corner-stone of a building. Stones – unless you are still in the stage of primitive religion – are not magic: they do not mean things on their own account.

Greater control and consciousness mean greater flexibility and greater freedom. We have achieved a large measure of this flexi-bility and freedom in the case of the physical world; we have divested it of magic and evolved the language of scientific method to deal with it. But in the case of the inner psychological world – the world of politics, religion, and personal relationship – we are still slaves. Our actions, feelings and talk are compulsive and with-out conscious meaning; we serve them rather than vice versa. Thus we lament the lack of freedom in modern states, and the lack of co-operation and fellow-feeling in modern society; we lament the lack of understanding between human individuals, the tragedies of failure in communication, the apparent or real con-flicts of desires between various parties, and so on. Rather than pin our faith on whatever miracle-working spirit happens to be fashionable, we need to evolve languages for these unsatisfactory situations. It at once becomes obvious that the development of a language involves a practical and down-to-earth attitude, to-gether with a great deal of hard work. We need to regard it as essentially like determining the rules for a game or the rules of procedure in a law-court. To get good results – to play the game enjoyably, to dispense justice fairly – we do not need any very exciting qualities of personality. We need only to experiment sensibly in making up the rules of procedure, and learn them properly, and abide by them; after that, the course of the game or the trial is largely settled for us.

To imagine perfect languages to deal with every human situation is, of course, utopian. But we can make a start. At present we do little more than outline certain qualities which we think useful in solving human problems; thus we could include honesty and truthfulness, being able to express oneself, talking over a situation, and so forth. It is possible to think of methods of formalizing these qualities, of arranging the situation so that it is as easy as possible for people to use them. To take a common example, it is well known that on many committees honesty does not flourish, because many of the members are waiting in fear to see what other members think; a junior member does not wish to advance an opinion against his boss, other members may not wish to appear revolutionary or unorthodox to their fellows, and so on. In this situation it is useless to try and persuade the members to be honest and outspoken, to give their real opinions, or to forget that they are in a particular social situation. The whole point is to try to replace an existing language with a new one. The existing language of many committees is well known. The individual members speak (as it were) with a public voice, through a mask donned for the benefit of the group and their own public images: their private voice, often used in the lobby, is unheard in the committee-room. People are often unwilling to assume personal responsibility, and often committees reach decisions that no individual member, at least in his private role, would himself have reached. This is, then, an inefficient language. Now suppose we extend the principle of the secret ballot – itself a first-rate 'linguistic' invention for dealing with political situations. Suppose we devise machinery whereby each member can record his views and opinions, as well as his votes, anonymously – on a tape-recorder which makes no differentiation between the different speaking-voices of individuals, for instance; no doubt a cumbersome device, but one which would eliminate the dangers outlined above. Such an invention would produce a more efficient language.

This hints at the most important feature of a language dealing with human situations – the degree of objectivity or 'externalization'. Everybody knows that in such situations people interrupt other people, lose their tempers and shout, contradict themselves, misunderstand each other and so forth. Now imagine a series of devices and a formalized ritual designed to reduce this to a minimum. Imagine, for instance, a device through which each party spoke which went dead if his voice were raised above a certain volume or pitch; imagine that only one of these devices could operate at a time, only after the previously-used device had been switched off by the party who spoke last; imagine that the ritual included playing the whole conversation back through a recorder, giving people the chance to emend or alter what they wanted, and also – more important – the ability to hear their own words externalized by the recorder. Imagine further that the session could not be broken up before a certain time, and could thus be free from the sort of emotional interruptions that often interrupt such efforts, such as somebody walking out of the room in tears.

Naturally this is only one language-ritual, and would not be appropriate for the whole range of individual communication or understanding. We need to know a number of factors which the above language would disallow : thus, anger, rage, fear of someone else, and so on are all real factors which must be expressed somehow if they are to be dealt with. This points to the second important feature of a language – that it should be flexible enough to include all that we want in a particular situation. We need not confine ourselves to one language, however; indeed a good deal of our present difficulty is that we attempt to deal with an almost infinite number of human and social contexts in what appears to us to be – and in one sense is – only a single language. We use the same words for rational discussion, for bullying, educating, exhorting, praying, threatening, making love and countless other purposes. What we require is a number of different language-rituals to cover the variety of situations; and one of the most important matters is that it must be clear to everybody when a person is using one language-ritual and when he is using another. The inner intentions of human beings are hard to verify even for themselves, and this makes it all the more essential to establish, by social usage, what a person is doing – what sort of game he is playing – at any one time.

The existence of a greater number of conventions, however, would in itself make a great many human situations easier, just as conventions in bidding in the game of bridge, by their mere existence and recognition, allow the players to express a variety of meanings and intentions. It now becomes apparent that one considerable difficulty is going to consist of learning and teaching the language. It is easy to recognize when you want to tell your partner that you have no spade, or four certain tricks in hearts, but not to easy to recognize *what* you want to express about your own feelings or the behaviour of other people. Phrases like 'I am angry' or 'I am hurt', admittedly, are slightly less crude than a threatening gesture or a flood of tears, but they still cover a great multitude of varied feelings. We feel tempted here to talk about self-awareness and perceptiveness; we need to be able to feel and distinguish between, say, anger at someone else for thwarting us, and anger at ourselves for being unable to meet a particular situation. But, as with the young child learning the simple language of material objects, the existence of an already-established language goes a long way towards helping the individual actually to make the distinctions about his own feelings. Thus, given (say) three different words for 'anger', with carefully specified meanings, it would not be hard for any normal individual to distinguish the feelings within himself to which the three words were intended to apply. It is plain that a similar sophistication of language in reference to words like 'love', 'attractive', 'friendship', and 'fear', to name but a few, would be of immense value.

We are entitled to expect far-reaching changes in our general attitude to ourselves and other people as a result of new language-techniques. There are many features of our behaviour which we take for granted, but which are nevertheless compulsive, and which would disappear as a result of greater control. Thus we are accustomed to regard our 'natural' likes and dislikes, desires and aversions, loves and hates as unchangeable parts of our nature.

One man is powerfully attracted by tall, willowy blondes; another hates anyone else sleeping with his wife; another is frightened of cats; another dislikes bananas; another is addicted to cigarettes; another dislikes jazz; another has a penchant for high-powered cars. Some of these, it will be noticed, are commonly regarded as 'normal' features, others as unusual, others again as signs of mental illness. But this sort of classification is nearly always done only by reference to a particular society; and it is in any case irrelevant to the question of free or compelled behaviour. All of them are cases where men are under the influence of magical symbols. To one man tall, willowy blondes 'mean' something in a language which he does not understand, the pseudo-language of his own unconscious mind; to another his wife is symbolically a possession, something which he alone can or should use; to another cats symbolize something frightening, and so on.

There may of course be different levels of awareness, different levels of language, in any case of compulsive choosing. Thus it is possible for someone to like high-powered and glossy cars without being aware that they are status-symbols; it is possible for him to be aware that they are status-symbols and be aware of why he is influenced by status-symbols; and so on. We require a different language to cater for all these cases. At present we try to make do with a single language, which operates moderately well for the object-world of physical reality, but which begins to come apart at the seams when we talk even about shallow sociological factors such as 'status', 'class' and 'communication' in a simple sense, and which fails almost totally if we want to take a look at and control the factors dealt with by depth-psychology, such as the origins of the need for status or of sexual choices. Given such languages, languages which will map out the most basic factors of our personality and subject them to the scrutiny of our consciousness, our will, our intentions and our reason, we may hope for infinitely greater flexibility of behaviour. No longer will certain types of women, certain foodstuffs, certain physical objects or certain behaviour-patterns come to seem compulsively preferable or compulsively intolerable. We should be able, as the psychologists keep telling us, to 'accept reality' for more fully what it is, for we should then have reduced more of it to linguistic form.

We do possess some languages for mapping our unconscious minds, besides the language of psycho-analysis. They are the languages of the various art-forms. As a method of control they are hopelessly incapable; indeed, in so far as the conventional signs used by them are rarely agreed or consciously understood (though they are artificial), it is perhaps strictly incorrect to call them languages, in our restricted sense, at all. In general they are stimuli, which move us, often profoundly; but there are some agreed conventions which can, by common consent as it were, affect us in certain ways, evoke certain types of feelings and enable us to put them on the map. Thus the use of a minor key in music, or a certain type of sentimental story, or certain emotive symbols in poetry, can by common consent evoke certain specific feelings or moods. As used in art-forms, of course, these forms are not so much symbolic of certain feelings as evocative of them – though they are artificially evocative. Their chief function as language, from our point of view, is that they do at least enable us to *identify* and face feelings which we might otherwise not identify and face, or at any rate not so clearly. Some degree of externalization has been achieved.

Moreover, they do something to bridge the horrifying gulf between the language of psycho-analysis and the wholly non-linguistic and uncritically-experienced feelings of everyday life. As has often been noticed, the difficulty with psycho-analytic language is that its statements are systematically difficult to prove; not in the sense that it is hard to collect evidence, but in the sense that the meaning of the statements is unclear. There is a gulf between the word 'want', say, in a statement like, 'Every boy wants to kill his father', and any conscious experience of wanting in the average person. In order to bring their points home in an effective way, psycho-analysts have to refer to case-histories, novels, plays and so forth – to a language or a pseudo-language which, though it does nothing to explain or even perhaps (in a strict sense) describe, can nevertheless evoke more subtly and specifically than the crude terminology of psycho-analysis.

Questions
1. In what sense do parrots 'talk'?
2. Do any words *stand for* things?
3. French, English, the Morse code, Roman numerals, the mating-call of birds; are all these 'languages' in the same sense?
4. 'The language of painting.' What could this mean?
5. How does language give us more control over the world?
6. 'Black clouds mean rain', 'This means war!', ' "Chien" in French means "dog" ', 'Cadbury's means good chocolate'. Discuss the differences of use in the word 'mean' in these sentences.
7. What is the proper function of conventions?

Philosophy at the University and Elsewhere

I THOUGHT IT useful to add some notes on the general position of philosophy in higher education and elsewhere; but this position is constantly changing, and what follows will inevitably be over-simplified. Once you have grasped the particular skill of philosophy (in the sense used in this book), you will be better able to make your own inquiries and draw your own conclusions.

In the Introduction (p. 1) I may have made it sound as if the word 'philosophy' was only used for the particular skills, approach or method dealt with in this book. For most academic circles in Britain, the U.S.A., the Commonwealth countries and some others, this is true. But it is not true elsewhere. Our kind of philosophy is often called 'analytic' or 'linguistic' philosophy, and distinguished from other kinds. Most of these other kinds of philosophy, like Marxism or existentialism, don't really involve special skills or techniques at all; 'philosophy' here means a set of particular beliefs about morals or politics or life in general. When people ask, 'What is your philosophy?' they use the word in this sense; they mean, 'What is your outlook on life, what are your personal beliefs?'

Hence in most universities and other institutions outside Britain, the U.S.A., the Commonwealth countries, and some others, the study of philosophy is what I would call 'history of ideas'. Thus in Paris you may study the thought of Sartre, in Moscow the thought of Marx, in Peking the thought of Mao Tse-tung, and so on. Not much is done by way of investigating the *meaning* or the *truth* of what these writers said; it is more a matter of getting a general grasp of their outlooks on life and their moral and political views. This may be profitable and interesting, but it isn't what *we* would call 'philosophy'.

In Britain, the U.S.A., etc., universities are mostly concerned with our kind of philosophy. Even here, though, there are two other things which we haven't touched on in this book : both of them might come under the general title 'philosophy', but they are best regarded as useful side-lines or additions to the kind of philosophy we have been talking about :

(1) There is the study of formal logic, and of the way in which different kinds of arguments work. This can be very useful, both for getting clearer about language and arguments in general, and also for pinning down the truth or falsehood of particular arguments.

(2) There is the study of the writings of past philosophers; the purpose is not to study them merely for their own sakes, but rather to help you to get clearer about particular problems. (Thus, what Aristotle and Plato wrote is not only of interest as part of the 'history of ideas' or because it is relevant to Greek culture, but also because these authors deal with philosophical questions which still puzzle us, questions like, 'Do we have free will?', 'Is there an absolute right and wrong?', and so on.)

Most universities do not like undergraduates to study philosophy full-time. They may let you spend most of your time on it, but there will usually be some other subject also. This is quite sensible, because prolonged and full-time philosophical thought is very difficult, and it's often a relief to have another (perhaps simpler) subject as well – preferably one which has a solid basis of *fact*, which philosophy hasn't got. Different universities combine philosophy with many other different subjects – history, languages, mathematics, science, and so forth.

One good way of telling whether you want to do philosophy or not is to see whether you're interested in the philosophical problems that arise out of other subjects. For instance, if you do geometry, you might find yourself wondering about the status of Euclid's axioms – are they self-evident truths, or just rules which define a game, or what? Or if you do languages, you might wonder about whether you could have a language without nouns (you couldn't, but why not?), and what a language really *is*. Or if you do science, you might wonder about what was meant by 'scientific method', or how we really know scientific laws to be true or false.

Philosophy can arise naturally out of most subjects (perhaps not woodwork or domestic science) but it's more immediately relevant to some than to others. If you're going to do rather vague* subjects, like sociology or psychology or literary criticism, then you ought to do some philosophy as well, because many of the difficulties with these subjects are really conceptual difficulties. On the other hand, it's quite possible to do (say) French, or ancient history, or biology, and some philosophy as well; the philosophy won't, in this case, relate very much to these other subjects, but neither it nor the other subjects will suffer from not being related. The choice here depends on whether you want the various parts of your university course to be interrelated, so that the philosophy you do is relevant to your other subjects, or whether you prefer to keep your different subjects separate. I myself would prefer a related course, like some of the courses offered at the new universities; but perhaps this is partly a matter of temperament, and I ought not to offer any particular advice.

Philosophy is increasingly studied at other institutions besides universities : at liberal arts colleges, colleges of technology, colleges of art and elsewhere. Partly because of the shortage of competent philosophers, the philosophy here is not usually of a very high standard; but it's worth keeping an eye open for anything that looks like philosophy in the prospectuses and brochures of such institutions.

From the point of view of getting jobs, the study of philosophy

* By 'vague' I mean only that they comprise a number of very different disciplines, and also that it isn't at all clear what these disciplines are and how they should be combined or related to each other.

is very much on a par with many other university subjects such as history or English literature. That is, they're not designed to lead immediately to a particular career, in the way that studying physics or engineering may lead straight into industry or some particular technological job. But a *good* degree in philosophy, as in any other subject, qualifies you for a great many jobs, and most employers are more impressed with the class of degree you have than with the subjects you take. If you're going to the university, or some other institution, primarily to get some particular technological job, then obviously it's silly to study philosophy as your main subject (though you can still do it part-time), but if you have no particular job of this kind in mind, then it will not be a disadvantage. The most important thing, in my view, is to make sure that you know what philosophy is, and decide whether you are interested in it and likely to do well at it. Your own interests and abilities are better reasons for choosing a subject than any other, both for your university career and for getting jobs afterwards.

Suggestions for Further Reading

I HAVE INCLUDED here only those books which I think may be useful for those beginning philosophy; they are not necessarily 'the best' books in any academic or scholarly sense. Beginners in philosophy usually suffer from too much reading and not enough thinking. At least it would be unwise to read the books below *until* you're quite certain that you've caught on to the basic skill – which I hope this book, and perhaps some of the books in section A below, will help you to do. On the other hand, when you really have mastered the basic skill, you can read quite a lot in a profitable (i.e. a critical) way.

SECTION A

Some introductions to philosophy, somewhat more difficult than this one, but still fairly simple :

John Wilson, *Thinking with Concepts* (C.U.P.)
E. R. Emmet, *Learning to Philosophise* (Longmans)
Susan Stebbing, *Thinking to Some Purpose* (Penguin Books)
G. J. Warnock, *English Philosophy since 1900* (O.U.P.)

SECTION B

Some books on particular philosophical problems which are reasonably clear and easy to read :

Aristotle, *Nichomachean Ethics* (Penguin Classics)
Plato, *Republic* (Bks I and II) (Penguin Classics); *Socratic Dialogues* (Nelson)
J. S. Mill, *Utilitarianism, Liberty, etc.* (Everyman)

S. Benn and R. S. Peters, *Social Theory and the Democratic State* (Allen & Unwin)

(Ed.) A. Flew and A. C. MacIntyre, *New Essays in Philosophical Theology* (S.C.M.)

John Wilson, *Logic and Sexual Morality* (Penguin Books)

R. M. Hare, *Freedom and Reason* (O.U.P.)

J-P. Sartre, *Existentialism and Humanism* (Methuen)

(Ed.) D. F. Pears, *The Nature of Metaphysics* (Macmillan)

This section could of course be extended much further. I have given only a small selection to start you off : the best thing is to find what authors are easy to read and helpful, and chase up the other things they've written. They will give references to other authors, and soon you'll get a clear picture of the right kind of books to read.